DO
THE TRUE
YOU

DO THE TRUE YOU

STOP FAKING IT FOR OTHERS AND FIND OUT WHO GOD SAYS YOU ARE

STEVEN FURTICK

NEW YORK   NASHVILLE

Copyright © 2026 by Steven Furtick

Cover design by Kristen Paige Andrews.

Cover copyright © 2026 by Hachette Book Group, Inc.

Hachette Book Group supports the right to free expression and the value of copyright. The purpose of copyright is to encourage writers and artists to produce the creative works that enrich our culture.

The scanning, uploading, and distribution of this book without permission is a theft of the author's intellectual property. If you would like permission to use material from the book (other than for review purposes), please contact permissions@hbgusa.com. Thank you for your support of the author's rights.

Faith Words
Hachette Book Group
1290 Avenue of the Americas, New York, NY 10104
Faithwords.com
@Faithwords/@FaithWordsBooks

First Edition: March 2026

Faith Words is a division of Hachette Book Group, Inc. The Faith Words name and logo are trademarks of Hachette Book Group, Inc.

The publisher is not responsible for websites (or their content) that are not owned by the publisher.

The Hachette Speakers Bureau provides a wide range of authors for speaking events. To find out more, go to hachettespeakersbureau.com or email HachetteSpeakers@hbgusa.com.

All Scripture quotations, unless otherwise indicated, are taken from the Holy Bible, New International Version®, NIV®. Copyright ©1973, 1978, 1984, 2011 by Biblica, Inc.™ Used by permission of Zondervan. All rights reserved worldwide. www.zondervan.com The "NIV" and "New International Version" are trademarks registered in the United States Patent and Trademark Office by Biblica, Inc.™

Scriptures marked NKJV are taken from the New King James Version®. Copyright © 1982 by Thomas Nelson. Used by permission.
All rights reserved.

Scriptures marked KJV are taken from the King James Version (KJV): King James Version, public domain.

Library of Congress Cataloging-in-Publication Data

Names: Furtick, Steven author
Title: Do the true you : stop faking it for others and find out who God says you are / Steven Furtick.
Description: First edition. | Nashville : Faith Words, [2026]
Identifiers: LCCN 2025045384 | ISBN 9781546009672 hardcover | ISBN 9781546009689 ebook
Subjects: LCSH: Self-actualization (Psychology)—Religious aspects—Christianity | Christian life
Classification: LCC BV4598.2 .F875 2026
LC record available at https://lccn.loc.gov/2025045384

ISBN: 9781546009672 (hardcover), 9781546009689 (ebook)

Printed in the United States of America

LSC-C

Printing 1, 2025

For Elijah, Graham, and Abbey.
It never stops!

CONTENTS

Introduction: The Trap, the Treadmill, and the True You..... 1

1: The (K)new You 9

MINDSET (01)
I'M NOT STUCK UNLESS I STOP.
ACTION STEP: COMMIT TO PROGRESS.

2: It's Not That Simple 21
3: Don't Argue for Your Limitations 31
4: Defy Your Default 39
5: Do the Thing That You Would Do 47

MINDSET (02)
CHRIST IS IN ME. I AM ENOUGH.
ACTION STEP: ACCEPT YOUR SELF.

6: More Than What You're Missing 59
7: Tricks Are for Kids 69
8: I Am What I Am 77
9: Coming from Abundance 85

MINDSET (03)

WITH GOD THERE'S ALWAYS A WAY, AND BY FAITH I WILL FIND IT.

ACTION STEP: FOCUS ON POSSIBILITY.

10: Forward, Not Finished 95

11: Now Move 103

12: Weasel-Free Mentality 113

13: What if This Succeeds? 121

MINDSET (04)

GOD IS NOT AGAINST ME, BUT HE'S IN IT WITH ME, WORKING THROUGH ME, FIGHTING FOR ME.

ACTION STEP: WALK IN CONFIDENCE.

14: That Lizard Is Loud 135

15: Don't Say That 147

16: God Is Up to Something Upstream 155

17: Make Peace with Your Strength 163

MINDSET (05)

MY JOY IS MY JOB.

ACTION STEP: OWN YOUR EMOTIONS.

18: The Hard Work of Happiness 175

19: Who's in Your Head? 185

20: A GR8FUL Heart Is a Stable Heart 193

21: Ugly Trust 205

MINDSET (06)

GOD HAS GIVEN ME EVERYTHING I NEED FOR THE SEASON I'M IN.

ACTION STEP: EMBRACE YOUR NOW.

22: Look to the Left 217

23: Help Me Fail 227

24: Found Fishing...................................233

25: God Chose You...Will You? 241

Conclusion: Step by Step, Day by Day 249

Acknowledgments 253

DO
THE TRUE
YOU

INTRODUCTION

THE TRAP, THE TREADMILL, AND THE TRUE YOU

THE TRAP

A week before my oldest son, Elijah, left for college, he asked me a question: "What's the best advice you can give me right now?"

To be honest, no profound answer popped into my head. The very idea of giving him "the best" advice freaked me out a little, as if I were being asked to condense the world's wisdom into a sentence.

I don't know the best advice, but I do know what the worst advice would have been: "Just do you."

Okay, maybe it's not the absolute worst answer in the world, but it's up there. Why? Because "you" is someone you haven't fully met yet.

"Doing you" is about being yourself—but do you really know yourself when you're fourteen? Or eighteen? Or eighty, for that matter? What you know about yourself is mostly made up of your life experience so far, which can lead to a lot of assumptions about the way things are and always will be.

If you overcommit to your idea of who you are today, it closes you off to what you could become tomorrow. That's the problem with the mentality of "just do you."

It doesn't set you free. It keeps you frozen.

It's not self-awareness. It's self-sabotage.

It's not the truth. It's a trap.

Now, don't get me wrong here: I'm not saying *don't* do you. I'm not saying to be somebody else, to fake it, to put on an act, to twist yourself into something other people tell you to be.

Being your authentic, unique self is a great goal to aim for and a healthy place to be. It's liberating to stop constantly comparing yourself to others, so I'm all in favor of self-acceptance. Of course you should be yourself. Who else would you be?

> In the pursuit of being you, don't settle for the you that you've always known.

But in the pursuit of being you, don't settle for the you that you've always known. Don't say, *This is just who I am. I'm a failure. A screwup. An anxious person. A depressed person. Insecure. Shy. Disorganized. Lame. Dumb. Not enough.*

Those labels are traps, and they sell you short. You're far more than your weakness or mistakes.

On the other hand, you're also more than the talents and gifts you've developed so far. Maybe you'd say, *I'm an athlete. I'm a musician. I'm a people person. I'm smart. I'm funny.* You are—but that's only the beginning. There's more to discover, more to learn, more to become. If you "just do you," you run the risk of only doing part of you.

God sees so much more.

Can you?

THE TREADMILL

Sooner or later, most of us realize that "just doing you" isn't enough. Who we've been up until this point can only get us so far. I'm sure there are some things about yourself you want to tweak, and a few others you want to completely transform. I know that's true for me.

So here's what we usually do. We escape the "do you" trap by climbing onto the "future you" treadmill.

What is future you? It's you—but with more friends, bigger muscles, higher grades, better skin, more followers, greater faith, and more success.

Future you is the shiny, perfect version of you. It's who you wish you could be. Who you think you should be. Who you would be if you just tried a little harder.

Or so you tell yourself.

The problem is, you never quite catch that version of you. But don't worry! There's always another product, diet, social media influencer, church service, or New Year's resolution promising that *this time*, you'll really become future you.

So you stay on the treadmill, running in place, chasing a goal that's just out of reach. Days, weeks, months, and even years slip by, but you can't enjoy them because you're desperately pursuing the person you think you should be. The person you will be proud of. The person who will finally be worthy of acceptance, love, and success.

Often, the mirage you're chasing doesn't even come from inside you. It's more like a mash-up of everyone else's strengths and successes that plays in your head on repeat.

You only see their highlight reel, though. It's not the true version of them, and it shouldn't define the true version of you.

If *doing you* is a trap that keeps you from growth, *future you* is a treadmill that kills contentment. When you constantly believe you need to become something you're not, you can't be happy with who you are today, and you might spend your time and energy trying to produce something that God never put in you in the first place.

THE TRUE YOU

So, if *doing you* has left you stuck, and *future you* has left you discouraged, where should you turn? Where should the pursuit of self-identity and self-acceptance lead you?

To the *true you*.

The you God created you to be.

The person he knows, sees, and believes in.

That person includes who you are today, but it isn't stuck there. And it includes many of your dreams and desires for the future, but it's not frustrated just because you're not there yet.

I believe with all my heart that God wants you to see yourself as he sees you—and then live out your God-given identity. That is the heart of this book: to help you align your mindsets with God's vision for you so you can be the most authentic version of yourself.

The true you is still unfolding to you, but it is fully known by God. He met that version of you because he *made* that version of you. He knows what he put in you and what he's calling out of you.

I love the story of how God first called Jeremiah to be a prophet. At the time, Jeremiah was young—likely a teenager—and he was having a tough time seeing past the person he had been up to that point.

God told him, "Before I formed you in the womb I knew you, before you were born I set you apart; I appointed you as a prophet to the nations" (Jeremiah 1:5).

Jeremiah didn't see himself as God's messenger to the world, though. He thought he was too young, too weak, too introverted, too scared.

So he pushed back. "Alas, Sovereign Lord, I do not know how to speak; I am too young" (verse 6).

Notice what God had already told him: "I knew you *before*."

He knew Jeremiah before he was born. Before the world hurt him. Before people mocked him. Before fear silenced him. Before he believed the lies in his head about what he could and couldn't do.

So God said, "Jeremiah, listen to me. I imagined you. I formed you. I set you apart. I'm calling you, and I'm going to be with you. What more do you need?"

When Jeremiah caught a glimpse of the true version of himself, the God-created version, it changed everything.

It will do the same for you.

Get this deep into your mind and heart: God knew you *before*. He knew you before you were born. He knew you before this world got ahold of you. He knew you before anxiety set in. He knew you before false accusations threatened you. He knew you before you were abused and abandoned. Long before the mistake, the failure, or the addiction, God said, "I knew you."

He.

Knew.

You.

He knew your parents would split up. He knew you'd feel invisible sometimes. He knew you'd go through heartbreak. He knew your friend group would split up and you'd be left on the outside. He knew you'd struggle with your self-image. He knew your brain would be wired differently from other people.

He knew it all and he saw it all. And he declared, "I have plans for you. I have a place for you. I have a purpose for you."

The you he sees is the one who is still kicking, still holding on, still going strong. The you just waiting to break free. The you who is coming up alive. The you this world won't corrupt. The you who drama didn't distract and trauma couldn't kill.

You were fashioned and formed by a God whose creativity knows no end. He says that you were fearfully and wonderfully made, that he knit you together in the womb, that your days are written in his book. He is a God who counts the stars and calls them all by name. He numbers the hairs on your head and sees the life span of every sparrow. His knowledge of you is as specific as it is infinite. It encompasses everything from hairs to sparrows to stars, so it

> You were fashioned and formed by a God whose creativity knows no end.

definitely includes you—every part of you, including the parts you don't know yet and the parts you called a mistake.

God knew the true you before he created you, like he knew Jeremiah, and he is calling the you he knew to come forward to the surface. You're the same person, but it's a new version, a fresh take, a greater understanding, a fuller experience, and an expanded definition of you.

You might not see it all yet—but God's seen it since day one. And now he's calling you to step into the true you.

Are you ready to get out of the trap of "just you"? Out of the thought patterns and default settings of who you've been up until now?

Are you ready to get off the treadmill of "future you"? To stop making yourself miserable by measuring yourself against an impossible ideal, an unrealistic version of a person God didn't create you to be to begin with?

It's possible. But it's not always simple. The true you is always trying to break through, but there's a tension and a struggle when you leave the old, false you behind. You have to choose every day to see yourself differently.

It's a tension I'm all too familiar with, and that's the heart behind this book. I'm going to share six mindsets, six affirmations, to put deep into your spirit. I want you to have a voice in your head that sounds more like the Holy Spirit and less like your old habits. Think of them as six downloads from heaven to update your mind and refresh your life.

Some of it might feel unfamiliar to you, but it's been in you all along. It just hasn't taken root yet. Some of it you're already doing, but God wants you to experience more of it.

I wrote this youth edition thinking specifically of the

challenges you might be facing trying to find your way in a chaotic and uncertain world. Family, school, friends, dating, mental health, life choices, college plans, a future career—it can all seem so overwhelming at times. No matter how old or young any of us are, we need the right voices in our heads along the way.

Throughout the writing process, my three kids—Elijah, Graham, and Abbey—have kept me honest. As I write these words, they are nineteen, seventeen, and fourteen years old, and they have no problem telling their dad when something is boring, confusing, or cringey. As I watch them navigate the madness that is adolescence and grow into strong, caring, mature teenagers and young adults, I'm in awe of what God can do for each of us. In fact, throughout the book, they are each going to pop in from time to time and share some of their own personal experiences with each of these mindsets. Not because they have mastered them—any more than I have. But hopefully their reflections will help trigger some of your own.

The advice I would give each of my kids is the message I'm excited to share with you: Don't settle for just "doing you." And don't waste another day chasing "future you."

The true you is not waiting in the future.

You can walk into it right now.

ONE

THE (K)NEW YOU

The other day I was driving to the recording studio for a songwriting session. I had a lyric in my head that I didn't want to forget, so I recorded a voice memo. It went like this: "Jesus, please be patient with me. I'm so far from the person I want to be."

Just as I finished singing that line into my phone, somebody cut me off in traffic. Without thinking, I yelled, "Idiot!"

The guy didn't hear me, of course—but my phone was still recording. So now I had a voice memo that went, "Jesus, please be patient with me. I'm so far from the person I want to be. IDIOT!"

It wasn't my finest moment. Ironically, I couldn't even write a song about being a work in progress without losing my temper at a bad driver, which proved how much I still needed to grow.

Have you ever been in a situation like that, one where your expectation of yourself didn't quite match up to reality? It's like you catch a distant glimpse of who you want to be, of who you could be—but then a different version of yourself shows up and ruins the vibe.

I've learned that every day, I face a choice. Which version of me will show up today? Will it be the me who is wiser from the mistakes of yesterday, or the me who is stuck in hurt or regret? The me who resists temptations, or the me who whispers to myself, *No one will know; it's not that bad*? The me who yells at dumb drivers, or the me who keeps my mouth shut and my temper under control?

You face the same choice. Which *you* will you do?

You make this decision every moment, in every situation, in every relationship, at the open door of every opportunity and the closed door of every disappointment. The Bible puts it this way:

> You were taught, with regard to your former way of life, to put off your old self, which is being corrupted by its deceitful desires; to be made new in the attitude of your minds; and to put on the new self, created to be like God in true righteousness and holiness. (Ephesians 4:22–24)

Notice that the passage mentions an old self and a new self. In other words, there is an old way of doing you, and there is a new way of doing you.

Here's what I want you to see: The you God knew from the beginning is the new you, the true you. He's inviting you to choose that version of yourself today.

Imagine yourself free from depression. God knows *that* you.

Imagine yourself filled with peace. God knows *that* you.

Imagine yourself overcoming habits that sabotage you. God knows *that* you.

This doesn't mean the "old you" was some horrible, awful worm of a person. This isn't a book about hating yourself. But the old you wasn't you at your *best*.

It was you surviving. It was you reacting. It was you living according to what you always believed about yourself.

There's so much more to you than that.

You have a version of yourself in your mind, but it might not be the vision God has for you. If today's version of you doesn't match God's vision for you, it's time to come up higher. It's time to learn how he sees you and who he created you to be.

Ask yourself: *What does God know about me that I don't know about myself? What does God see in me that I've overlooked or even denied? God has chosen me, but have I chosen myself?*

Nobody else can be that person: only you. That's why comparison is such a trap. You aren't trying to become like anyone else. Why would you sell yourself short like that? Work on becoming like *you* instead.

> You aren't trying to become like anyone else. Why would you sell yourself short like that? Work on becoming like *you* instead.

ELIJAH

I feel like every kid going through middle and high school struggles with comparison. I know I sure did (and lowkey definitely still do).

When I was in kindergarten through sixth grade, I went to a super tiny school. I'm talking, like, twenty people would be considered a big class. Then, in eighth grade, I switched to a way bigger school. I remember walking in on that first day like it was yesterday. I saw everybody wearing all these crazy fits, and immediately I started questioning myself. I realized whatever drip I thought I had was nonexistent.

Right away, I started switching up how I dressed to impress my new friends. But one of the best things my dad has ever told me is this:

"You can care about what people think, but you can't let it control you."

So, the older I've gotten, the more I've realized that nobody really cares about what's on your feet. It's the swag that's inside you that really attracts people. And if you stay true to yourself, you'll make whatever you're wearing look good.

I'm not going to sit here and say I never compare myself to other people now, but what I can say is the more I remind myself of what God has put in me, the more I realize he's already given me more than enough.

Now, I'm not saying you can be or do anything you imagine. If you're 5'4" and you stopped growing two years ago, you're probably not going to play in the NBA. I think that is a healthy limitation to embrace. But I can tell you with confidence there is more to who you are than what you've experienced up until now, and God wants to give it to you.

You have to say yes to the process, though. You have to choose to do the *true* you.

Stop saying, "This is who I am, so get used to it," and instead say, "This is who I am *so far*, but I'm not dead yet, so God's not done yet. I'm still growing. I'm still changing. I'm still learning. I like a lot of things about this edition of me, but I don't like all of them, and I'm not stopping until I become who God says I can be!"

As you begin to walk out the "true you" version of yourself, it will become natural. You'll find yourself saying, "I guess I *am* a patient person. I *am* a kind person. I *am* a brave person. I didn't used to feel that way, but I'm seeing it more and more now."

Doing the true you is always more about God's grace than your grit. The Bible says that you are what you are by his grace, and his grace is powerful (1 Corinthians 15:10). Grace is God's patience with you and his power in you. Thank God for grace!

> Doing the true you is always more about God's grace than your grit.

Let me be clear, though. Grace is patience *and* power. Grace is never an excuse to be lazy or a way to avoid change. That's the polar opposite of what I'm saying. Sometimes you hear people use grace as a cover-up to keep doing wrong behavior. "I'm just a sinner saved by grace," they say, as if grace means they never need to change.

No, grace is the means by which God changes us into the

people he knows we can be. It comes from him but it flows through us.

So, when you have an outburst of anger, find yourself gossiping about others, look at porn, manipulate and lie to get your way, or hold on to a grudge until it eats you up from the inside—remember that's not who God is, so it can't be who you really are, and his power is at work in you to change.

Now, it may take a while for the version of you that God knew all along to become the version of you that you know in your everyday life. And to be honest, in some ways you'll always struggle with the switch.

I know I do. I'm not writing this book because I've got it all together. I can find myself snapping at the people that I love because my emotions are burned out. I can preach on Sunday about God's grace and power in our weakness, then get depressed on Monday morning because I don't feel like I preached well enough.

Instead, I'm writing because of my struggles and my belief in a God who gives victory step by step. I'm writing this because I'm determined to get better at being a dad, a pastor, and simply a person.

Sometimes I'm glad to be me, sometimes I'm proud to be me, and sometimes I'm embarrassed and scared to be me. But "me" is all I've got. And you know what? It's who God wants. I'm not who I want to be yet, but I'm not giving up either.

Ephesians 4 makes it sound so simple: Just put off the old self and put on the new. It's like coming home, taking off your school clothes, and sliding on your favorite hoodie.

I wish putting off the old self was as easy as taking off a shirt, but it feels more like struggling out of a straitjacket. I wish putting on the new self were as simple as throwing on a sweatshirt, but it takes hard work and dedication to build new habits.

The point is constant progress, not instant perfection. Real transformation comes by making lots of small, right choices that line up with who you are in Christ.

> The point is constant progress, not instant perfection.

That's why I want to walk with you into this new you, almost like a coach would do, with these six mindsets. You can say these things to yourself wherever you go. Whether you're pulling an all-nighter to finish a project, going to an audition or tryout you're nervous about, or just trying to survive until the end of the school day, what you say to yourself changes you from the inside out.

Each of these truths is very personal to me. These are the things I repeat to myself when I'm going to preach on Sunday morning, or when I'm trying to get my act together as a parent, or when I'm just pulling myself out of bed on a Monday morning. I preach these things, I pray these things, I say these things, and I believe these things for you and for me.

With each of these mindsets, there is a call to action that God will enable you to take. It's one thing to say you are forgiven and free, but it's another thing to live that way, and these action steps are meant to give you clear direction.

I'm going to share the whole list with you now, just to give you a preview before we move forward.

1. *I'm not stuck unless I stop.*
   Action Step: Commit to progress.
2. *Christ is in me. I am enough.*
   Action Step: Accept your Self.
3. *With God there's always a way, and by faith I will find it.*
   Action Step: Focus on possibility.
4. *God is not against me, but he's in it with me, working through me, fighting for me.*
   Action Step: Walk in confidence.
5. *My joy is my job.*
   Action Step: Own your emotions.
6. *God has given me everything I need for the season I'm in.*
   Action Step: Embrace your now.

I'm getting fired up just listing these declarations! I hope you are too. In fact, if you can, say a few of them out loud right now. See how they feel coming out of your mouth. Maybe even type them in your phone or make them your wallpaper. They are meant to be easy to memorize, like a song or a slogan would be. I want them to be like tracks on repeat in your heart so your faith can work in real life.

Remember, though, that if you think you have to fix yourself in order to get God to love you more, you're starting from the wrong assumption. *You'll never be more loved than you are right now.* You'll never be more accepted than you are this instant. The work of Jesus settled that once and

> *You'll never be more loved than you are right now.*

for all. You don't need to stress and strive to somehow prove yourself to God. God is close to you, and he blesses you, and he is proud of you, and he is cheering you on *right now.*

You are the one God loves. That needs to be your starting point. But where you start isn't where you have to stay. That's why I'm so excited about these six mindsets. When you choose to think and live in these ways, you are choosing *you.* You are deciding to overcome distraction and discouragement so you can experience all that God created you to be.

I know this to be true: Wherever you are on your journey, God has good things planned for you. I'm not saying you won't face challenges or make mistakes along the way, but I believe God sees good days ahead for you. He has prepared good works for you to do. His calling is your confidence, and his grace is your guarantee.

The *knew* you and the *true* you are the same you, and they are the right you. They are the best version of you. They are God's version of you.

The first mindset we're going to look at is the foundation for all the rest: *You aren't stuck unless you stop.* Why does this matter so much? Because without a commitment to progress, you're defeated before you start. But if you can get deep into your heart and mind that you serve an unstoppable God who is leading you forward, no distraction, deception, difficulty, or devil can stand in your way.

MINDSET (01)

I'M NOT STUCK UNLESS I STOP.

**ACTION STEP:
COMMIT TO PROGRESS.**

TWO

IT'S NOT THAT SIMPLE

A while back, my son Graham was competing at a wrestling tournament, and I was in the stands. There was a lady behind me who was cheering at the top of her lungs for a team called the Spiders. Unfortunately for her, the Spiders were getting crushed. (Literally, because that's the point of wrestling.)

This particular match I was watching was in the heavyweight division, which goes up to 285 pounds. The boy who was winning was every bit of those 285 pounds, while the Spider trapped underneath him was definitely not. No matter how hard the smaller kid tried, he couldn't move.

From behind me, I heard the woman yelling at the underdog: "Get up! Come on, just stand up!"

The kid on the wrestling mat couldn't hear her, but if he could have, can you imagine how he would've responded? Absolute sarcasm, I'm sure.

"Oh, yeah! I forgot! *That's* what I'm supposed to

do—*stand up*. Thank you, lady in the bleachers, for reminding me. I'll just go ahead and do that now."

We all know it's not that simple to "just stand up" when you're getting crushed by life. In moments like that, the last thing you need are condescending voices telling you to do exactly what you're already trying so hard to do.

You feel like yelling, "If it's so easy, why don't you try it? Why don't you get down here on the mat and see what it's like being me? Why don't you try getting bullied every day? Why don't you try having to split your time between divorced parents who fight all the time? Why don't you try dealing with the social battleground called high school? Why don't you try crippling anxiety?"

When you're stuck in a rut, in a bad habit, in a toxic relationship, in depression, in discouragement—you don't need shame and blame. You don't need someone to roll their eyes and tell you to just get up and get over it. You need someone who understands your situation to be with you in it and to encourage you through it.

And that's exactly what God does.

God doesn't scream at you from heaven, "Get up! Do more! Fight harder! Sin less! Be better!" He doesn't shame you for dealing with hard things, because he knows what you're going through.

The Bible says this about Jesus: "For we do not have a high priest who is unable to empathize with our weaknesses, but we have one who has been tempted in every way, just as we are—yet he did not sin. Let us then approach God's throne of grace with confidence, so that we may receive mercy and find grace to help us in our time of need" (Hebrews 4:15–16).

A high priest was someone who spoke with God on behalf of the people. Here, the Bible is saying that Jesus knows exactly what you're going through because he lived it too.

It gets even better. Not only does God understand your struggle, but he's fighting alongside you. Life isn't a high school wrestling match, after all, and you don't have to fight alone. In your time of need, God's grace and strength are yours to lean on.

Now, I know this can be hard to believe if you just got dumped by your boyfriend, or if you're trying to stop vaping but you can't, or if you recently found out your uncle has Stage 4 cancer. When you are stuck under a 285-pound problem, giving up can feel like the only option.

But it's not.

This is what I want you to get deep into your heart and your mind: *You're not stuck unless you stop,* and you don't have to stop because God is with you in the fight.

> You're not stuck unless you stop, and you don't have to stop because God is with you in the fight.

I'm not saying your problems aren't real or don't matter. This isn't about gaslighting yourself into thinking things are fine even when the world is falling apart around you. Instead, it's about choosing to trust that God has a way to move you forward, even when you feel stuck.

That's what the *true you* would do.

The true you—the real you, the God-created you—is aware of problems but committed to progress. That means taking small steps forward, even if you don't have everything figured out yet. It means asking for help if needed. It means getting creative and trying new things.

I remember when I turned sixteen, and all my friends were getting their driver's licenses. I didn't want to take the test. I avoided it. I put it off. I made excuses. Not because I didn't think I could drive safely, but because I have a terrible sense of direction, and I was afraid of looking stupid. I figured that as long as I couldn't drive, I couldn't get lost.

It was pretty ridiculous because the town of Moncks Corner, where I lived, was really small. It wasn't a one-stoplight town, but it wasn't Manhattan either. Yet somehow I had convinced myself that I was going to make wrong turns and embarrass myself. So I didn't get my license.

Do you want to know how I finally did it? My dad came home from work on a lunch break one day in the middle of summer. (My birthday is in February, which tells you how long I let fear keep me locked up.)

He said, "Get in the car."

"Where are we going?"

"You're going to get your driver's license. I'm tired of driving you all around, and so is everybody else. You're not going to sit around my house all your life telling me you need a ride. You're going to get your driver's license."

I said, "I can't do it."

"Well then, you'll fail. But you can't drive now anyway. So if you fail and you still can't drive, what have you lost?"

That day, I got my license.

I had convinced myself I was stuck, but really, I had just stopped. And within a few weeks, even though the car we could afford was pretty cheap and badly needed a paint job, I was giving one of the prettiest girls in eleventh grade a ride home every day.

It's funny how quickly you can go from overwhelmed to excited. All it takes is a glimpse of the next step. It can work for you anytime there's something you feel like you can't do, but you know it's necessary.

See, stuck is a way of saying you can't move forward and *there's nothing you can do about it.* When you're stuck, your circumstances have taken control. Things are hopeless and you are helpless, so you might as well quit trying. It's a frustrating, powerless feeling.

But that's not how God operates. That's not even his nature. He's not a frustrated, powerless God, and he didn't create you to live a frustrated, powerless life.

God is the Waymaker. He is all-powerful and all-knowing. He causes valleys to be raised up and mountains to be made low. He turns graves into gardens and bones into armies. Our God is a sea-splitting, stone-rolling, wind-whispering, fire-from-heaven, water-from-the-rock, stop-the-moon-in-the-sky kind of God.

When you feel hopeless, he is nearer than ever. In those moments when your story seems stuck and hope is lost, God will make a way for you. He wants to give you back your courage, your power, your peace.

I could list a hundred times I've said I was stuck, but I wasn't—I had just stopped. I had stopped thinking about the problem creatively and started self-sabotaging and freezing up with fear. I had stopped praying and asking God to show me my next step. I had stopped strategizing with the help of the Holy Spirit, and I was walking within the limits of my own abilities and experience.

It's important to realize that you can expect to put *work*

into moving forward. Your problems usually won't disappear the moment you say a prayer. You should plan on knocking on a lot of doors and asking a lot of questions. Keep talking to God about what you're facing. No matter how many times you've asked him about your current situation, you can keep asking. No matter how many times you've brought it up before, you can keep coming to him. That's part of faith.

Jesus said, "Ask and it will be given to you; seek and you will find; knock and the door will be opened to you. For everyone who asks receives; the one who seeks finds; and to the one who knocks, the door will be opened" (Matthew 7:7–8). There's no shame in asking, seeking, and knocking. It doesn't mean you're doing something wrong or that God fell asleep on the job. It just means you're putting in the work to get to where you need to be.

But if you don't *believe* you can move forward, you won't ask or seek or knock. You'll just sit there, miserable and suffocating under 285 pounds of weight, wishing you were somewhere else while people in the cheap seats holler at you.

Now, keep in mind that the way forward might not look like what you expected. God's idea of progress and his definition of success don't always make sense to us at first. Sometimes we get so caught up in our expectations of what we think is supposed to happen that we don't recognize the doors God is opening right in front of us. How often do we miss an opportunity because our idea of what should happen is too narrow? Too small? Too human?

The way forward might not look like what you expected.

Maybe God hasn't healed an injury or illness you're dealing with, but that doesn't mean he's abandoned you. It doesn't mean your faith has failed. He is doing other things in you and through you. His grace is sufficient for you.

Maybe you bombed that college entrance exam, but that doesn't mean your future is over. God has something else ahead, but you might have to pivot. Remember when Jesus' disciples fished all night and caught nothing, and then Jesus said to try again—but this time, to cast their net on the other side of the boat? Cast your net on the other side. Try something new. Do something different.

ABBEY

Recently, I was in a situation where I felt stuck and was forced to pivot. Pivoting can honestly feel so uncomfortable when you are in it. Casting your net on the other side isn't easy when you've been fishing on the same side for as long as you can remember. It takes so much trust.

A year ago, my parents and I made the decision for me to switch schools. Anyone who has had to switch schools knows how nerve-racking that can be. Not only is your whole environment different, but you have to meet all new people and make so many adaptations. At that time, the switch felt like a punishment. It was hard for me to see how anything good could come from leaving everything I knew and was comfortable with. I didn't want to cast my net in another location. I wanted to stay in the place

> that was familiar—where I already had friends and a life.
>
> This reminder that what I might initially see as a punishment can actually be a reward in the Lord's eyes encouraged me to take a step of faith and embrace my situation. If I had given up and stuck with what was familiar to me, I never would have received the new people and experiences God was putting in my life. I was blessed with new friendships that I made through sports and classes, and I received many opportunities to learn and grow that I wouldn't have experienced if I hadn't pivoted. It gave me a whole new perspective on change and obstacles and reminded me of all the things God can see that I can't.

Don't give the obstacle you're facing or the failure you've experienced too much credit. No matter what has made you feel stuck, God is bigger than that thing, and he's already on the other side of it. It's not the end of the road. It's just a curve you can't see past. Maybe it's even a fork that will open up new opportunities. If you give up now, you'll never know what miracle God has just ahead.

> If you give up now, you'll never know what miracle God has just ahead.

Say it to yourself: "I'm not stuck unless I stop! I might be temporarily slowed down. I might be facing something I've never faced before, something that seems too big for me. I might have to rethink, recalibrate, reset. But God is on my side. I can go to his throne of grace in this time of need. God is bigger than my battle. He's in control of this situation. He's greater than my circumstance, so it's only a matter of time before I find the way forward!"

That might not be how people around you treat their obstacles, and it might not be how you've faced yours in the past. But you're doing the true you now. You're stepping into the you who God sees, and that version of you is committed to progress.

THREE

DON'T ARGUE FOR YOUR LIMITATIONS

My dad grew up in a rough household. His own dad—my grandfather—was an alcoholic, a mean drunk who physically abused his family. Then, on my dad's seventh or eighth birthday, my grandfather died by suicide.

Those things affected my dad a lot. He decided to break the cycle with his own kids, and he worked hard to give us opportunities to succeed.

He was passionate about this. I remember when I was in high school, somebody told me I would never be able to afford college. My dad didn't even graduate from high school, so that triggered him. He shut the person down.

"Don't say that! Don't ever tell my boy he can't go to college. I'll rob a bank if I have to. I'll kill somebody and take their money to pay for him if he wants to go to college."

Obviously you shouldn't use robbery and violence to pay for college—but his response meant a lot to me. It sent me a message: "Don't let my limitations become your insecurities.

It might be my history, but it's not my legacy. You can do something different."

That's a message we need to keep telling ourselves. When it comes to getting rid of limitations that hold us back, passion is a good thing. We need to get aggressive.

Instead of that, though, I sometimes find myself doing the opposite—I argue for my limitations, not against them. I defend them. I make excuses for them.

I once heard a motivational speaker named Les Brown say, "If you argue for your limitations, you get to keep them."

Think about that. It's tragic but true.

So why would I hang on to something that holds me back? I think there are a couple of reasons.

First, some of my limitations have been part of my life for so long, I've started to believe they are part of me. They feel normal.

This is just who I am, I tell myself. It's almost like I'm so loyal to the false, incomplete me that I can't become the true me.

Second, it can feel painfully vulnerable to make changes. To take risks when I might fail. To put myself out there when I might make mistakes. To pursue a dream with no guarantee of success.

> Vulnerability is scary. Limiting ourselves often feels safer than believing in ourselves.

Vulnerability is scary. Limiting ourselves often feels safer than believing in ourselves, so we make arguments to "prove" why we can't do what God created and empowered us to do.

The mindset "I'm not stuck unless I stop" means you

don't let *loyalty* to a past version of you or *fear* of doing something new stop you from living up to what God says about you.

Do you ever argue for your limitations so well that you end up keeping them? Do you ever defend your idea of who you are to a God who believes in you more than you believe in yourself?

Maybe you're interested in a career path, but you won't even take the first steps to see if it's possible because you've already talked yourself out of it. *I'm not good enough at science to be a doctor. I'm not smart enough to be an engineer. Nobody in my family even went to college. Who do I think I am to dream of something this big?* So you give up before you even try. You argue for your limitations rather than against them.

Maybe you laugh off a bad habit by saying, "That's just my personality." Or you excuse a wrong decision because "Everybody else is doing it." Or you settle for a toxic relationship because you say, "This is all I can hope for. This is what I'm worth." Or you label yourself as stupid, as not enough, as a failure because that's the message you're getting from everyone around you, and you don't have the strength to fight it.

But God is sending you signs and signals that there is more in you. He wants to show you things you can do and places he'll take you.

Don't respond with, "I could never do that; I'll never be that." You'll sabotage your future before you even have a chance to try.

When you are being called by God to change, it can feel

like a betrayal of what you've always been, and that brings up all kinds of emotions. "Oh, no! If I'm not who they want me to be, they won't like me. If I say no to going to that party, they won't want to be my friend anymore. If I don't numb the anxious or depressive thoughts, I won't be able to handle them. If I don't do whatever it takes to get what I want, I won't be happy."

If you're going to do the true you, you can't be loyal to your limitations. You can't make a case for the things in you that are not like Christ. I'm not saying you should deny they exist, but a lot of us go far beyond recognizing our weaknesses—we actually defend them.

When the devil tells you that you're worthless, do you start collecting evidence to help him? Do you say, "That's right, I *am* worthless," and then list all the evidence that backs up that accusation? Do you go out and do things that make you feel even more worthless?

When you feel too tired or overwhelmed to face a problem that comes up, do you agree with those feelings? "I'm too stressed out for this. Life is too much. I might as well give up."

I think we need to add another sentence to that motivational phrase. "If you argue for your limitations, you get to keep them. *But if you agree with God about your potential, you get to grow into it.*"

What potential? The potential God sees in you. The doors he is opening for you. The gifts he has given you.

If God says you can change, you can change. If he says you can be an example for your friend group, you can be a leader. If he says he put something in you, then he can call it out of you.

Is your limitation shouting louder than your potential? Because you won't *move* past it until you can *see* past it.

You have to catch a vision of the version of you that God sees, because that vision will pull you out of what you're stuck in and propel you toward what you were created for. Once you agree with God about what he sees in you and what he says about you, you'll stop fighting your future.

> You have to catch a vision of the version of you that God sees.

As I mentioned already, fear of failure is one of the biggest motivations behind our arguments. We often defend the way we are because we're afraid that if we try to change it, we'll fail—and failure seems like a worse outcome than staying stuck.

I remember a stand-up comic who was talking about learning to perform in public, and he said something to the effect of, "You've got to bomb if you want to get better. You've just gotta get up, bomb in front of an audience, then realize, *Oh, that happened, and I didn't die. People moved on and forgot about it.*"

Fear of failure can be such a loud voice in your head that you never take the next step. In the moment you face what you fear, though, God strengthens you for it.

Be willing to put yourself out there and do what you believe God is calling you to do, even if you bomb once or twice. Then you'll realize, "Oh, that wasn't so bad. I was freaking out about all these things, but God was already at work. I can do this. I've got some work to do, but I can't imagine going back to the old me now."

Listen to God's arguments *for* you or you'll be persuaded by your own arguments *against* you every time. You'll let the devil's lies and the world's labels define you. They can't see the true you, though. Only God can—but you have to agree with him.

There's a story in the Bible about Moses sending twelve spies ahead of the Israelites into the Promised Land. The people wanted to check things out before they entered, and Moses went with it. So, off they went. They came back saying, "We seemed like grasshoppers in our own eyes, and we looked the same to them" (Numbers 13:33). They saw themselves as small and weak in comparison to the people who lived in the land. They argued for a grasshopper self-image, and they lived a grasshopper existence in the wilderness for the next forty years. They thought small and stayed stuck.

The following generation had a different mindset, though. At some point, they rejected the way their parents thought about themselves and God. That doesn't mean they were disrespectful, but they drew lines. They learned. And they leveled up.

Then, when Joshua sent two more spies to check out the land, they came back with a totally different report: "The LORD has surely given the whole land into our hands; all the people are melting in fear because of us" (Joshua 2:24).

The new generation looked at the same land, the same enemies, the same risks—but they had a different mentality. They knew they weren't stuck unless they stopped. They agreed with God about their potential, and that set them up for victory.

What if you are the new generation? What if God is calling you to have a different mentality than what you've seen before? What if you're the one who can stand in courage and change the way you see and talk about yourself? What if the true you is ready to step forward into all God has for you with full confidence?

Now, the old version of you got you this far, so don't hate it. Just don't defend that version when it comes time to change. Your past failures and successes are part of who you are today, but they don't get to decide who you will become.

> Your past failures and successes are part of who you are today, but they don't get to decide who you will become.

Agree with God and commit to progress. Say, "All right, God. I don't know if I see myself this way, but you do. You think I have what it takes, and that's why you let me face this situation. You obviously know something about me that I don't, so I'm going to step up. I don't want to see myself as small anymore. I want to see myself the way you do. I'm going to rise to the level of your expectations, not sink to the level of my experience."

Ask yourself: Am I arguing for my limitations or my potential? Am I defending what I've always done or developing what God says I can do? Am I agreeing with my fear or with my future?

It's a choice you make. It's a mindset you put on. You're not stuck unless you stop, so agree with God and commit to progress.

FOUR

DEFY YOUR DEFAULT

About ten years ago, I started to notice that none of my pants fit anymore. For a while, I wore joggers every day because I was in denial about my expanding waistline, but I finally ended up paying a tailor to adjust my pants and make them bigger.

I remember looking at the guy and saying, "I hate this! I could be spending this money on a lot of other things. Instead, I'm paying you to make my clothes bigger."

He said, "Keep eating! It's job security for me."

Up to that point, I had tried different exercise plans and diets, but without a lot of success. I would always tell people, "I hate exercise. I don't like to work out. I don't like to lift weights. I did back in high school, but I don't like going to the gym now. That's not me."

That was my default.

Eventually something clicked inside me, though, and I began to rethink my attitude toward exercise. I decided to defy my default.

I turned a room in my house into a workout space. I started with just a bench, some adjustable BowFlex dumbbells, and a treadmill somebody gave me. I put a little Bluetooth speaker in the room because I figured lifting weights would be less painful with classic rock blaring in the background. Then I talked several of my friends into coming over and working out with me four days a week.

I even named the workout room. I called it the POUND. It's an acronym: The Place of Ultimate Natural Development. I know, it's epic. Sometimes it takes epic (and a bit cheesy) to get you motivated every day to do something you don't want to do.

I told my workout partners, "Guys, I'm not an exercise person, so I'm not doing chin-ups. I'm not doing burpees. I'm not doing squats." I set the bar low because I wasn't sure I was actually going to change.

I hung a chart on the wall, and every time I worked out, I put a star on it because I thought that would reinforce the behavior. It did, even though I felt a little silly. I was a grown man with a beard putting stars on a chart like a seven-year-old.

That was many years ago, and I still work out several times a week. A while back, I added up all the star charts, and I was surprised to see I had worked out over three thousand times. And yet just the other day, I was talking to somebody about exercise, and I caught myself saying, "You know, I'm not really a workout person..."

Then I stopped myself. I realized that, yes, actually, I *am* "a workout person."

I didn't used to be. I didn't think I was. I never saw myself that way before. But now I am someone who loves working out and who does it consistently. Why would I deny or downplay it? It's something I enjoy, it's a good example for my kids, and it's healthy.

I'm not saying this to brag. I'm not trying to sell you protein powder or a gym membership. I just want you to see how hard it can be to defy your default.

After all the work I had put in, I still saw myself the same old way: as someone who wasn't strong, wasn't consistent, wasn't committed in this area of my life. Even after two thousand stars on the chart.

I *was* a workout person. That was my new default. And I needed to believe it.

So when did the switch happen? When did I become an "exercise guy"? Was it workout 522? Workout 1396? I can't really tell you, because it doesn't really work like that. There wasn't one moment where I suddenly became that kind of person.

But somewhere along the way, star by star, the limited version of me became a truer version of me. The weaker version became a stronger version. And I like this version better.

We don't know what we'll enjoy, what we could be good at, or what we could grow into. We don't always know who we are, even as we are becoming it.

But God does.

In order to do the true you, you have to challenge the old you. The default you.

> In order to do the true you, you have to challenge the old you.

This is where the mindset "I'm not stuck unless I stop" takes on a deeper meaning. It doesn't just apply to overcoming obstacles and solving problems. It also applies to the process of *inner* growth—of becoming who God made you to be.

When God called Joshua to lead Israel, he knew Joshua needed to see himself differently than he had up until that point. So God challenged him to confront his default way of thinking. "No one will be able to stand against you all the days of your life. As I was with Moses, so I will be with you; I will never leave you nor forsake you. Be strong and courageous, because you will lead these people to inherit the land I swore to their ancestors to give them" (Joshua 1:5–6).

I think Joshua was struggling with some self-doubt. He had just taken over from Moses, the guy who led Israel out of Egypt and through the desert, so he had big sandals to fill. And he was supposed to lead Israel into the Promised Land, which was an impossible goal unless God did a whole lot of miracles.

Joshua's default seems to have been fear and insecurity. His default was to be second-in-command, not the leader. He probably saw himself as less than others, as not enough, as too timid or too young.

But it was time to challenge those default settings and step into the true Joshua, the Joshua who God had known since the beginning of time.

What does God see in you that you can't see in yourself? What defaults do you need to defy? Where have you been stuck so long that you've assumed this is who you really are and who you'll always be?

Maybe when you argue with your parents, your default is to get angry and storm out of the room, followed by the silent treatment. Maybe when you're around other people, your default is self-doubt or fear, so you don't speak up when you know you should. Maybe your default is suspicion, so you have a hard time trusting people or building good friendships. Maybe your default is to lose your temper, and people around you never know when you're going to blow up. Maybe your default is to put others down instead of finding the good in them and building them up.

One of my defaults that I've had to work on is how I take criticism. I remember going on a mission trip to China when I was in college, and my leader told me, "Steven, your biggest problem is that you're defensive."

I responded, "No, I'm not!"

Ironic, right? I got defensive about being called defensive.

But I don't have to do that. I can choose to listen. I can take some time to think about criticism instead of punching back. I can say, "Let me think about that. Let me get back to you." And then I can bring it to God and ask him to help me see where I'm being defensive and how I can choose a different response instead.

Do you see how this works? As I let the confidence of Christ shape how I see myself, I begin to defy my default, and I grow into something I never knew I could be.

This takes self-awareness. It takes work. It takes courage and humility. And most of all, it takes time.

Then, somewhere along the way, you become "that person." That patient person. That kind person. That relaxed person. That pure person. The person God saw in you even when you never saw it in yourself.

Was it kind word 522 that did it? Was it good decision 1396? No, of course not. It doesn't work like that with your maturity any more than it does with your muscles.

But it does work. You do change.

The Bible says we "are being transformed into his image with ever-increasing glory, which comes from the Lord, who is the Spirit" (2 Corinthians 3:18). It's a process, and God's in charge. Let him set the pace.

As you pursue the true you, you'll need to defy your default time and time again. You'll find yourself caught between your comfort and your calling; between what you've always done and what God is inviting you to do next.

This can feel unnatural at first, but that doesn't make it wrong. I remember trying to learn how to play tennis, and the first thing the instructor told me was, "Show me how you hold your racket."

I showed him, and he moved my hand to a completely different position. The next few weeks sucked because I felt like a four-year-old every time I served. The ball went everywhere except where it was supposed to go.

With practice, I got better. I'm not going pro anytime soon, but I did improve.

At first, though—and this is so important—I got worse.

That's the thing about defying your default. When you first try, it feels unnatural, awkward, difficult. You don't get it right, and that can be embarrassing, even discouraging. You might be tempted to give up because the learning process shows you how far you still have to go.

But with the Holy Spirit as your coach and mentor,

growth isn't just possible. It's inevitable. Just don't give up too soon.

Are there areas of your character, your attitude, or your actions where you need to defy your default, even if it feels a little awkward at first? Are there circumstances in your life you've accepted as normal that you need to fight to change, even though there is some resistance? Is God calling you, like Joshua, to grow into a new version of yourself that feels a bit intimidating?

> With the Holy Spirit as your coach and mentor, growth isn't just possible. It's inevitable.

Your default is not your destiny. It's just a starting point. It's where you are today and it's how you act right now.

But you are growing. You are changing. The struggle itself is your Place of Ultimate (Super)natural Development. You're not working out your abs; you're working out your faith. You're living out your identity, and you're being transformed into the image of God through Jesus.

As long as you don't stop, as long as you don't settle, as long as you don't make excuses for a version of yourself that is beneath the one God knew before the beginning of time, your default can't define or deter you. You are being transformed each day into the image of God in you.

That's the true you.

FIVE

DO THE THING THAT YOU WOULD DO

When I was twelve years old, my greatest wish was to be in a rock band. I dreamed about it. I obsessed over it. The only problem was that I didn't really play any instruments and neither did my friends.

But I didn't let that stop me. I made up fake bands. I would come up with a cool-sounding band name, then I would go to a friend and say, "Yo, man, you're in my band. You're my drummer."

And he would say, "What are you talking about? I don't play the drums. I've never taken a lesson in my life. I don't even have a drum set."

"It doesn't matter. You're the drummer in my band."

Then I'd go find a bass player who didn't play bass, a lead singer who couldn't sing, and so on. I would even create fictional CDs for my imaginary bands.

Then one of my friends, Michelle, told me about a guy who played bass. By that time I was getting better at the guitar, but I still didn't have any friends who could be in a band. So I asked her, "Does he really play bass?"

She said, "Yes."

I said, "Does he own a bass?"

"Yeah."

"I want to meet him."

We started a band together. Eventually his brother joined, and we had a legitimate three-piece band. We named our group Deadbeat. We'd perform anywhere anybody asked us to go, as long as they had enough electrical outlets and nobody kicked us out for making too much noise. We didn't get signed by any labels—not even close—but my rock band dream had come true.

I laugh at twelve-year-old me now. How weird is it to start a fake band and put out fake albums? But it didn't feel weird to me at the time. I didn't have a real band, so I just did what I would do if I *had* a band—until I got one.

> When you aren't where you want to be yet, do the thing that you *would* do if you were already there.

Here's my point: When you aren't where you want to be yet, do the thing that you *would* do if you were already there. Or at least get as close as you can.

In other words, ask yourself what you *would* do if you didn't have a limitation, an obstacle, a giant standing in your path. Then do whatever you can to head in that direction, even if it's only a tiny step, and even if you don't know what you're going to do when you get there.

Do the thing you would do if you knew God was making a way forward.

That's commitment to progress.

And that's how you get unstuck.

Success doesn't come through superhuman feats of strength or by finding shortcuts nobody else knows about. Success is found in every step you take in the right direction, even when the destination isn't guaranteed or the dream seems far away.

Maybe you say, "If I had an hour free every day, I would learn to play the guitar." But you don't have an hour—you only have ten minutes. Well, practice for ten minutes. If learning the guitar is the thing you would do if you had more time, do a mini version of that thing.

Maybe you say, "If I had better grades, I'd apply for college scholarships." Start sending out college applications anyway. Look for other kinds of scholarships. If college is your dream, take a step toward it, even if you don't see a clear path forward, and see what happens.

The idea is to start moving in the direction you want to go, even if all you can manage today is a small, imperfect step. Those small steps add up.

This is about working with what you've got. Use what God has put in your hand, no matter how unlikely or limited it is. Do the thing that you would do, even if it's only a preview, a practice round for the real thing.

Now, this phrase, "Do the thing that you would do," actually has a double meaning. It doesn't just mean do the thing that you *would* do if you weren't facing the obstacle or limitation in front of you.

After reading Ephesians 4, it also means "Do the thing *that* you would do."

Which you?

That you.

The true you. The one who God knew since creation. The version of you he is calling you to step into now. *That* version of you is the real you, the authentic you.

So when you're facing a tough choice or situation, do the thing that *that* you would do.

Are you facing comparison and peer pressure? Do the thing that the confident version of you would do—the one who knows they're perfectly made by God and doesn't need to prove their worth.

Are you struggling with temptation? Do the thing that the Spirit-led you would do. The you who chooses the right road, not the easy road.

Are you worried about a relationship that seems like it's falling apart? Do the thing that the gracious, loving version of you would do: listen, forgive, and act in wisdom.

Are you frustrated by a delay? Do the thing that the patient version of you would do. Take whatever steps you can take and leave the rest to God.

"Do the thing that you would do" is a strategy to break out of lethargy. It's a way to focus your faith when you feel confused or unsure how to proceed. It's a challenge to come up higher. It's a call to faith.

So spend time with God and get his vision of the you you're becoming—then start living like that person now. Don't act out of your old self, your old patterns. Act your way into your new, true self with the power of the Holy Spirit. That you *is* you, so start doing that you.

> Spend time with God and get his vision of the you you're becoming—then start living like that person now.

Would *that* you pray? Then prayer is the thing that you should do right now. Would *that* you show up on time to school? Then being on time is the thing that you should do. Would *that* you tell the truth? Turn off your phone and be present? Say you're sorry? Stand up for somebody who is being bullied? Refuse to gossip? Choose love?

Then do that thing. And then the next thing. And then the next.

A few years ago, before my father passed away, he and I went through a rough time in our relationship. He had been diagnosed with ALS, a terminal disease, and between his failing health and some medication he was taking that affected his moods, things were really difficult. We would get on the phone and try to talk to each other, and we would both end up yelling. Whenever I called him, he would go into a rage within two minutes.

This went on for months. It was terrible. On Sundays I would get up and preach to my church, and on Tuesdays I'd have a shouting match with my dad. I felt like a hypocrite about it, but I couldn't figure out a way past it.

I knew what I wanted: reconciliation. I wanted to be by my dad's side. I wanted to be able to take care of him. The problem wasn't knowing what needed to happen. It rarely is. It was knowing how to get there. The issue was figuring out how to move forward in an impossible situation. I had tried everything I could think of, but we seemed to be stuck in anger and dysfunction.

Father's Day rolled around. I happened to be driving home from a vacation with my family. I remember being lost in thought as I drove, feeling bad that I couldn't be with my dad but also furious and hurt at how he had been treating all of us, especially my mom. Suddenly something my father-in-law had told me weeks earlier popped into my head. "Try to remember the good times. He did a lot of things right."

As I was driving down the same highway that went through the town where my dad lived, Moncks Corner, I had an idea. I wasn't sure if it was a good one or not, but it was something I hadn't tried yet, and I wasn't ready to give up. I didn't want my dad to die without our relationship being restored, and I didn't know how much time I had left.

I asked Holly to drive, and I pulled out a piece of paper and a pen. I decided to write down one good memory for every year he had been my dad. I was thirty-two, so that meant listing thirty-two things.

I wasn't sure I could do it, to be honest. That's how mad I was. Even though he was a good dad and did far more than thirty-two positive things, I didn't know if I could remember that many. I was going to try, though, and I was going to drop off the list at his house when we drove through.

At first, I could hardly get a word on the page. My mind was full of all the abusive things he had said and done in the last few months, and it took a lot of effort to rewind the clock and think about my childhood. But as I moved the pen across the page in faith, as I did the thing that I would do if I had a good relationship with my dad, the good memories and feelings began to flow.

The first thing I remembered was when I played baseball as a kid. Dad was our coach, and we were so bad, he wouldn't let any of us swing when we got up to bat. He made us bunt for the whole season. So I wrote down one word: "Bunting." That got me started.

Then I remembered a time when I was about fourteen years old and he took me to a punk rock concert in Ladson, South Carolina. He liked fishing, not punk rock, but he was trying to connect with me, and he knew I loved music. The concert was the worst music we had ever heard, but we were there together. I wrote down, "Punk rock concert, Ladson."

Now it was flowing. Next I remembered a time he took me to a revival meeting at a little country church. The guest speaker was an old-school fire-and-brimstone preacher, and we were seated in the front row. The preacher got really fired up, and people started hollering. At one point a little boy jumped up and shouted, but he didn't say, "Amen" or "Preach it, preacher." He yelled, "Let the wild hog eat!" I had never heard that one before, and to be honest, I still don't know what he meant. I wrote it down. "Let the wild hog eat."

I finished the list just as we pulled into Moncks Corner. We drove up to the house, and I knocked on the door. I didn't even hug my dad when he opened it. I just handed him the paper. "Here. I made you a list. It's thirty-two things I remember about you."

I wish I could say we hugged and fixed our relationship right then, but this wasn't a Hallmark movie, and we were too stubborn and hurt by each other to do that. All I did was hand him the list, sit with him for ten minutes, and walk back to my car.

He called me later and asked, "How did you remember all this stuff?" We talked and laughed for a few minutes. It was a crack in the wall between us. It was a tiny way forward, and we both took it.

Not long after that, we truly made peace with each other. I was able to be with him when he passed away a few months later. I will forever be grateful that God didn't let me stop trying, that he kept nudging me forward even when I felt trapped.

As I think back over that Father's Day breakthrough, I see the power of this principle: "Do the thing that you would do." By making that list, I did a mini version of the thing that I would have liked to do, which was to be able to talk with my dad. But since we couldn't talk without shouting, I wrote. I did the thing that I would have done if we both weren't so hurt, or at least something that pointed in that direction. It was hard, and I really didn't want to do it at first. But I'm so glad I fought my initial feelings and was obedient to what I felt God had asked me to do. The lasting result was greater than the temporary emotion.

The second meaning of the phrase "Do the thing that you would do" is even more important, though. I had to choose to act like "that me," the true me, the God-created me. The list the current version of me wanted to write would have been titled "32 Ways You've Let Us Down in the Last Two Years" or something like that. But that's not the version of me I wanted to take into my dad's final days. It's not the version of me I knew God could see. So by his grace, I did the thing that *that* me would do. I chose humility. I stirred up love. I took a risk. I tried one more time.

And God came through.

That's what gives me hope in every difficult circumstance, and it's what should give you hope too. You may not always be creative or strong or determined or holy or selfless or giving—but *God* is.

He is what you need. He has what you lack. When you turn to him, you find the grace to step into a more mature, more patient, more capable you. The true you.

> God is what you need. He has what you lack.

As long as there is breath in your body, God is going to keep nudging you forward. He's going to remove the layers of your old self and replace them with your true nature. He's going to challenge your defaults and expand your ability to handle pressure. He's going to show you who you really are and lead you into the future he has always known.

You can't do it without God—but God is not going to do it without you either. His power is flowing through you. His hand is leading you. You will be enough for the task at hand because Jesus makes you enough. You're not stuck unless you stop, and you're not going to stop because he is leading you forward.

This connection between Christ and us lies at the heart of our second mindset, our second affirmation, which might be the most important one of all: *Christ is in me. I am enough.*

MINDSET (02)

CHRIST IS IN ME.
I AM ENOUGH.

ACTION STEP:
ACCEPT YOUR SELF.

SIX

MORE THAN WHAT YOU'RE MISSING

It was the 2016 Olympics. The final match for women's wrestling was moments away from starting.

In the tunnel leading to the arena, twenty-four-year-old American wrestler Helen Maroulis was waiting to compete. Next to her was her opponent, Japanese competitor Saori Yoshida. Saori was a three-time Olympic champ with thirteen world gold medals to her name, and she was the clear favorite to take home the gold today. Helen had competed against Saori Yoshida twice before at past events—and lost both times.

But she had been training for three years for this moment.

"I've never felt anything like what it felt like before the finals match. It was electric," Helen remembered in an interview later. "I look over for one second, and I see Yoshida, and I turn back. I'm like, *Oh dang, Helen. Oh man.* Five seconds is enough for a bad thought to get into your mind or a negative thought or a doubt or anything. I'm like, *God, how do I protect myself right now?* So I had this mantra: Christ is in me. I am enough. Christ is in me. I am enough."

Minutes later, Helen defeated Saori Yoshida 4–1. It was one of the biggest upsets in wrestling history.

I love that story for two reasons. First, my son is a wrestler, so I respect an Olympic gold medalist to the highest degree. Second, the mantra Helen kept repeating to herself is something I preached about a few weeks before she won the Olympics, and she watched the sermon online. Knowing that Helen found strength in an affirmation from a sermon—and then won Olympic gold—made me smile.

Whether you're an athlete going to the Olympics or a student heading into finals week, it's all too easy to lose focus. To let negativity creep in and take over.

In those moments, you need to know how to talk yourself *out* of some things and *into* others. You talk yourself out of doubt and into faith. Out of your weakness and into God's strength. Out of your head and into your future.

You don't face an opponent on a mat; you face obstacles in life. You face the opposition inside your own mind. And instead of fighting once every four years, you find yourself wrestling every four *minutes* with another reason to doubt yourself. Another reason to wonder if you are enough. Another voice telling you to be stronger, smarter, funnier, prettier, taller, thinner, richer, cooler, nicer.

Sometimes—maybe a lot of the time—you might feel overwhelmed by it all. You're trying to juggle school, friends, family, dating, goals, college plans, mental health, and more, but you're dropping more balls than you catch. Or at least it feels that way.

ELIJAH

There's been so many times when I've felt alone or doubted myself, and honestly, I feel like most of it comes from social media. It's like every time I open my phone, I'm hit with this constant flood of other people's success, happiness, and highlight reels. It started when I was younger—I remember one night in eighth grade, sitting in my room scrolling through Snapchat. I saw some of my boys hanging out without me on their private stories. The thought hit me immediately: Maybe I'm not really part of that group. Those kinds of thoughts can completely hijack your brain in a second.

And that hasn't gone away as I've gotten older. Now it's celebrities, influencers, and people my age showing off how "perfect" their lives are.

A wise man once said in his sermon, "We compare our behind-the-scenes to other people's highlight reels," and that stuck with me. When I get caught in that cycle, I start doubting myself. I overthink my future, wondering how I'll ever measure up or get to where all these people seem to be. I start to feel small, like I'm not enough.

But what I've learned—and what God continues to teach me—is that I'm not on this journey alone. God is on my side. He's already gone ahead of me and planned every step, every moment, in ways I can't even imagine. My timeline isn't supposed to look like anyone else's. When I start to slip into that

> comparison trap, I remind myself: God's plan for me is good. I don't have to have it all figured out. I just need to trust him.

I think we've all heard an inner voice of failure, of worthlessness, of not being enough. I know I have. Too many times I've found myself struggling to manage eighteen things at once, and none of them can be ignored because they all matter.

But I can't do it all. I don't have enough time. I don't have enough energy. I don't have enough patience. I don't have enough...

The list of "not enoughs" never ends.

Even worse, it's an easy jump from "I don't have enough" in a few areas of your life to "I am not enough" as a person. The first is just a statement about the situation you're going through. The second is a label that locks you into an old version of yourself.

In other words, you might start to see yourself based on what you're missing. You turn your insufficiency into your identity. You make your lack into your label.

Now, I'm sure you have good days too. I know there are areas where you are strong, times where things go right, victories that make you proud. Those moments are often glimpses into the true you, the version of you that God created you to be. Those moments are encouraging, but they will never make you feel enough. Not for long anyway. And they're not meant to.

Only God can do that.

That's why this mindset has two parts. "Christ is in me. I am enough." You can't have the second half without the first half.

Jesus told his disciples right before his death and resurrection, "Because I live, you also will live. On that day you will realize that I am in my Father, and you are in me, and I am in you" (John 14:19–20). A few verses later, he said this famous phrase: "I am the vine; you are the branches. If you remain in me and I in you, you will bear much fruit; apart from me you can do nothing" (15:5).

Jesus was telling his disciples that their lives were connected to him—and that was what made them enough.

Can you hear the encouragement in Jesus' voice? He wasn't yelling at them, "Be holy enough! Be wise enough! Be pure enough! Be perfect enough!" He was saying, "*I* am enough. And because I'm with you, you will be enough."

He says the same thing to you.

You are more than what you're missing. Your mistakes don't get to tell you who you are. You have nothing to prove because your value comes from Christ—and he's never going to let you down.

> You are more than what you're missing. Your mistakes don't get to tell you who you are.

ABBEY

My entire life, there has been this pressure to "fit in." It has always seemed like there was some type of standard I needed to live up to, and if I didn't fit in, I would be left out. But the thing about "fitting in" is that there are strings attached. The more you put your value in worldly things and start following the crowd, the more you start to lose your godly values.

I have learned over the years that it's better to be lonely for a season and still have your value in Christ than to follow the crowd and constantly feel convicted by the Holy Spirit. When you follow the crowd, you can feel like you're fitting in so well even when you're doing things you know you shouldn't. But you do it for validation. Then you get home and feel totally empty and guilty for sinning. You are filled with so much regret. While loneliness can hurt for a season, the dirtiness of sin stays with you much longer.

That's what I love about this mindset—Christ is in me, I AM ENOUGH! Even if you feel lonely, you have an everlasting friend who is with you every step of the way. When you find your worth in him, you are so much more fulfilled than you would be following the crowd.

I've found that my true self isn't a high school stereotype—it's my identity in the Lord. Your friends may give you a hard time about your mistakes, but the Lord never will.

Instead of blaming yourself, rejecting yourself, hating yourself, or running from yourself, you can accept yourself. Accept your true Self—with a capital S because it's the version of you that God created.

It's way too easy to start telling ourselves we aren't

enough. Most of the time, we don't even know we're doing it. The other day, my son Elijah told me he was planning a fishing trip with his friends. When I was a kid, my dad taught me to fish (or he tried to anyway), but I was bored the whole time. So, as a parent, I never took my kids fishing.

When Elijah said he wanted to go with his friends, my brain jumped from "Cool, he wants to fish," to "He doesn't know how to fish," to "I never taught him to fish," to "I'm a bad dad because I never taught him to fish."

All this took place in a split second. Do you see what happened there? Suddenly the fact that Elijah didn't know enough about fishing meant I wasn't enough as a dad.

Have you ever done that? You take an area where you don't measure up to some ideal of perfection and you turn it into a reason to hate on yourself. Then it all spirals from there.

"If I were a better friend, she wouldn't have stopped talking to me. If I were smarter, I wouldn't have bombed that math test. If I looked more like that girl on social media, he would have wanted to date me. If I made the team, my dad would have been proud of me. If I wasn't so much trouble, my parents might not have gotten a divorce. It's all my fault. I'm just not enough."

Obviously you're not perfect—nobody is. All of us could have made some better choices along the way. Show yourself some compassion, though. Maybe you are doing a really good job, but life has just been hard. You don't have to blame yourself for that.

I'm sure you've heard the Taylor Swift lyric that says, "I'm the problem, it's me." My daughter used to listen to the song all the time. I think some of us have that phrase on repeat in our heads. "I'm the problem. It's me. I'm not popular enough. I'm not friendly enough. I don't have enough focus, enough confidence, enough style, enough talent. Yeah, I'm the problem here. It's me."

Now, if you really are part of the problem, recognize it and work on it. You're not stuck unless you stop, remember? But my point is that you can't jump to dramatic, depressing conclusions about yourself every time you go through challenges or make mistakes. Accept your God-designed, God-created Self as God accepts you—then work toward a better result in whatever areas need to improve.

The point I'm trying to make is that if you want to stop the downward spiral of despair, you have to realize you are already enough in Jesus. His life is within you. He is providing the resources you need. "Enough" is not a state you will eventually reach—it is a gift you have already been given.

> If you want to stop the downward spiral of despair, you have to realize you are already enough in Jesus.

That's what God wanted Moses to understand when he described himself as, "I am who I am" (Exodus 3:14). He wanted Moses to see that his very nature is "enoughness." It's God's presence, not your performance, that makes you enough.

Do you really think God would just drop you into your life and not put within you the things you need for what he has called you to do? When you don't feel like you're enough, don't fall into the trap of trying to be everything and do everything on your own. Tell yourself, "I am enough because

God knew I would be here. He knew what I would need for this situation. If he put me in the situation, he put his strength in me."

As Helen Maroulis said, all it takes is five seconds for negativity and doubt to get into your head. So focus less on your lack and more on God's abundance.

God is enough, and he gives you enough and makes you enough. He fed Israel manna from heaven for forty years. He gave them water from a rock in the desert. He told ravens to feed Elijah during a famine. Jesus turned water into wine at a wedding. He had a fish pay Peter's taxes. He fed thousands of people from a little boy's lunch. He told the disciples exactly where to cast their nets and they pulled in the biggest catch they'd ever had.

I could go on and on. God isn't running out of resources. If he showed up for the men and women in the Bible, he'll show up for you. If they asked for it, you can ask for it. If they believed for it, you can believe for it. God gives you what you need, when you need it, so that you can do what he asks you to do.

I'll say it again. *You* are enough.

Not some ideal, impossibly perfect version of you. Not the person your parents wish you could be. Not the person you're pretending to be.

You. Today. Right now.

You are already accepted by God. You already have the mind of Christ. The Spirit already dwells in you. God's promises are already yours.

Don't say you're *not* enough; say you're *now* enough. That's how God sees you, and that's what Christ makes you.

You're not done growing, of course. You are being transformed into God's image every day, so there are some habits and immaturities you still have to leave behind. But in your essence, at your core, you are who you need to be because you are handmade by God. You are the handiwork of the divine. He made you on purpose. That is the you that you need to accept because it is the one who God made.

The God who knows you is the One who chose you, so you have nothing to prove, no one to impress, nobody to fear. He calls you by name. He knows the hairs on your head and the thoughts of your heart. He values you, loves you, fills you, empowers you. He sees the power and potential he put within you.

Do you?

SEVEN

TRICKS ARE FOR KIDS

When I was nine, my mom took me to the trading card shop in Moncks Corner, the town where I grew up. She waited in the car while I went inside and bought a pack of basketball cards. I was so excited, I opened the pack right there at the counter. Immediately I recognized the name on one card:

Michael Jordan.

The owner of the store was watching me. When he saw the Jordan card, he leaned over the counter and said, "Hey, I'll trade you another pack of cards for that one card."

That seemed like a no-brainer to my nine-year-old self. "A whole pack for one card? Sure!" I handed him the card, he gave me another pack, and I walked out of the store thinking I had gotten the best deal ever.

When I got back to the car, my mom asked how it went. When I told her I got two packs, she was immediately suspicious. "How did you get two? I only gave you money for one."

"You'll never believe it, Mom! He gave me a whole new pack for one card."

"Steven, what card was it?"

"Michael Jordan."

Her face changed immediately. She told me to wait in the car, then she marched into the store. Five minutes later, she came back with my Michael Jordan card—and a third pack of cards.

You see, my mom knew the value of that card. So did the owner. But I didn't, so I fell for a trick. I traded away something valuable because I was too young and inexperienced to recognize the worth of what I had in my hand.

I wonder, how often do we trade away our God-given identity because we don't know our own worth? We fall for the lie that we don't matter that much. The devil tells us we're broken beyond repair, and we believe him. The world around us says our worth is based on what we look like or how much money we have, and we believe them. Our own minds whisper that we are frauds and imposters, and we believe ourselves.

So we fall for tricks.

We give away what really matters and chase after what doesn't.

Instead of cards, we hand over our character. We hand over our calling. We hand over our confidence.

We lose our peace in the pursuit of pleasure. We exchange our joy for stress, our generosity for fear, our good reputation for five minutes of popularity.

I grew up in the eighties, and there was an ad campaign for Trix cereal that always repeated the catchphrase "Silly rabbit! Trix are for kids." It's true, if you think about it: *Tricks* are for kids. Immaturity and lack of experience are the things that con artists prey upon.

That's why I let go of a Michael Jordan card, and it's why we often let go of our Self: the person God says we are. If we don't see our own value, we'll get tricked into trading away our true selves for things that don't matter.

> If we don't see our own value, we'll get tricked into trading away our true selves for things that don't matter.

There's a fascinating story in the Bible about Jacob convincing his brother Esau to give up his birthright. As the firstborn, Esau would have been in line for leadership of the family and a double inheritance. But one day, he came home hungry after a hunting trip and saw Jacob cooking stew. Esau's stomach took over. He ended up trading his birthright to Jacob for a bowl of stew, which has to be the worst trade in history (Genesis 25).

Esau's desire to eat and his fear of dying got the best of him. He was immature and unwise. He was impatient. He was focused on what felt good, not on what was actually good.

So he fell for a trick.

It's easy to criticize Esau, but we do the same thing when we sell ourselves short by not valuing who God made us to be. That's why we have to continually grow in our knowledge of who we really are. And it's why learning to "do the true you" doesn't happen overnight.

Do you want to avoid tricks? Learn how valuable you really are so you don't settle for less than you were created to

> Learn how valuable you really are so you don't settle for less than you were created to be.

be. Hang out with people who will remind you of your true worth and reflect it back to you. Spend time learning what God says about you in the Bible.

Say it out loud: *Christ is in me. I am enough.* Put on this mindset. Change the way you see yourself and talk about yourself. After all, your voice is the one you hear the most often, and it's the one that affects you the most deeply.

Often, the tricks that trip us up are of our own making. We don't need the devil to lie to us: We're doing a fine job of it all on our own. "I can't do that. I'm never going to be able to do this. I shouldn't even try. I'll mess things up. Someone else would do a better job anyway."

To be honest, we often have good reason to be pessimistic: We live with ourselves. We have a front-row seat to our mistakes and bad decisions. If we focus only on that, and if we forget that Christ in us is what makes us enough, our weaknesses can convince us that we'll never be enough for what God has called us to step into.

I remember when I accepted Jesus at the age of sixteen. At first, I wrestled with the decision because I wondered if following Christ would cost too much. But when it came down to it, what's not to accept? Salvation is the best. Jesus paid for my sins. He took away my shame. He helps me when I'm weak. He prays for me when I don't have the words to say. Who wouldn't want that?

You know what's been a lot harder for me than accepting Jesus?

Accepting *Steven*.

Accepting Jesus took a moment; accepting myself is taking a lifetime. Steven is far from perfect. He loses his temper. He says dumb things. He struggles with fear and anxiety. He lets people down. He doesn't always know what to do. Every day I live with Steven, I discover a few more things I don't like.

Now, there's good stuff in me too. My wife says I'm an awesome husband, and I think my kids are pretty happy to have me as a dad. But as I said before, I'm so far from the person I want to be (IDIOT!). And the more I grow, the more I see how far I have to go.

I try really hard to be like Jesus. But at the end of the day, I'm still Steven.

What I've realized, though, is that if you accept Jesus but don't accept yourself, it's like believing the cross was big enough for the world—but not big enough for your flaws. You can't just accept Jesus by faith. You have to accept your *Self* by faith. Sure, you're a work in progress. But you are beautiful, valuable, and important right now too.

David wrote, "I praise you because I am fearfully and wonderfully made; your works are wonderful, I know that full well…How precious to me are your thoughts, God! How vast is the sum of them!" (Psalm 139:14, 17). David made some massive mistakes, but he knew how valuable his life was to God. He never forgot how much he was worth.

Do you know your worth? Do you value your Self? Have you accepted that you are valuable beyond description to God? Are you committed to loving your Self, showing grace to your Self, stepping into your Self, and trusting God with your Self?

Or do you see yourself as less than others, as not enough, as disposable, replaceable, forgettable? That's the message the enemy will try to give you—but it's not what God says about you.

At the card shop, the guy at the counter knew the value of his cards because he had a book that told him how much they were worth. If I could have looked up my Michael Jordan card in that book, I wouldn't have traded it away for a one-dollar pack of worthless cards.

You have a book that tells you *your* value. It's called the Bible. Have you looked yourself up in that book? Did you read the part where Jesus gave his life for you because you're worth so much to him? Did you see where it says that the Holy Spirit lives in you? Did you read that you have a calling and a future, that God has given you gifts that are unique to you, and you have to use those gifts because nobody else can do what you do?

> If you look yourself up in the book, you'll see that you are worth the world to God.

If you look yourself up in the book, you'll see that you are worth the world to God. You are more than a conqueror. You have the mind of Christ. You are chosen and called.

Don't settle for less than that!

GRAHAM

Something I have always wrestled with is my worth. I feel like most of my life I have gotten my worth from external sources like athletic ability or the voices of the people around me. But when I got into middle school and life became a little bit more real, these things started to tell me more negative things about myself than positive. When I wouldn't get as many likes on an Instagram post, I would start to think people didn't like me as much as they used to or maybe I was doing something wrong. Eventually these thinking patterns led me to have a very distorted view of who I am.

But at summer camp going into my junior year, my dad challenged the youth in our church to start reading a chapter of the Bible every day and watch how much our lives would change. I decided I would read one chapter every day and write down my thoughts about it. It became a habit in my life, and as I've learned about how God thinks of me, those external sources have lost all their value. Learning what God says about me has changed the way I live. It has given me an untouchable confidence. I no longer worry so much about what other people think about me because I know what the most important person thinks about me.

If you have made any trades that you regret, if you've let your character slip or your confidence weaken or your calling fade, it's time to reclaim the version of you that is rightfully yours.

The Holy Spirit will walk into the card shop for you. He'll tell the devil to give you back your peace, your joy, your dream, your kindness, your courage, your passion, your creativity, your song. They are part of the true you, and nobody can take them if you refuse to trade them.

Learn who you are in Christ, then step into that version of your Self. It's who you were meant to be—and it's perfect.

Don't let anybody tell you anything different.

EIGHT

I AM WHAT I AM

I remember taking a Greek course in college. It seemed like a good idea because the New Testament was written in Greek, and I figured that being able to read the Bible in the original language would be helpful.

Ancient Greek turned out to be ridiculously hard to learn. Within a few weeks, I knew I needed to cut my losses and drop the class. I was a mass communication major, not a religion major, so Greek wasn't a requirement.

So, one afternoon when classes were over, I walked into the professor's classroom with a slip from my adviser, who was helping me drop the class and switch to something easier. The professor was standing there with another teacher, and their response was, "Well, Furtick, we knew it wouldn't take long, but you dropped this class even quicker than we expected!"

They were joking around, but there was an undertone of "We knew you weren't a serious enough student to do this level of work."

Even though they were joking, their words stuck with me. To this day, I have a nagging voice in my head that tells me I'm not "serious" enough. Sometimes when I'm getting ready to preach, it's as if those two professors were standing there, taunting me in my mind, telling me to prove that I'm deep enough and disciplined enough.

I'm not saying they would think that about me today—this is all in my head. I get that. But my point is that sometimes things get into us more than we realize at the moment.

The things that hurt your self-acceptance don't show up in your life fully grown. They start as tiny seeds, as subtle ideas or comments that you don't even question at first.

Maybe a teacher told you in second grade that you weren't good at math, so you've given up trying. An ex-boyfriend made you feel like the breakup was your fault, and you believe you're bad at relationships. Someone in high school made fun of your voice and now you're self-conscious anytime you sing.

Years ago, my daughter, Abbey, told me she hated her ears. When I asked her why, I found out her brothers had said her ears were too big. So I tracked down her brothers. I let them know that kind of comment had no place in the Furtick household. Why? Because I don't want my daughter going around embarrassed about her *ears*, of all things. I don't want a little seed planted in her that turns into a self-image problem later in life.

You see, over time, seeds of self-rejection grow. You water them every time you agree with them, until eventually they turn into overgrown weeds that choke out who you really are. You end up despising parts of you because you fall short of what you "should" be.

But who gets to define what you "should" be? Shouldn't it be the one who created you? The one who chose you before time began, who loves you more than you love yourself, who knows you better than you know yourself?

> Who gets to define what you "should" be? Shouldn't it be the one who created you?

The mindset we're looking at, "Christ is in me. I am enough," is about more than just tolerating the person God made you to be—it's about celebrating who you are. It's about stepping into that version of you with full confidence and no apologies.

This matters because it affects how you handle challenges and opportunities. For example, if I'm constantly fighting a voice that tells me I'm not deep enough as a preacher, then all that defensiveness is going to come out in how I preach and teach. I'll subconsciously think, *Oh, this needs to be deep. I can't get on that platform and be shallow. I've got to prove to the people who said I'm not deep that they're wrong.*

That's not going to help at all, though. If anything, it will block me from hearing God. I will get in my own head. I will make it all about proving something instead of serving someone.

I know this is specific to my role as a pastor, so it might be a little hard to relate. But I bet you've experienced the same dynamic. Maybe someone laughed when you shared an idea, and now you second-guess yourself every time you speak in front of people. You constantly think they're looking down on you, laughing at you, expecting you to fail. So you stress out even more, trying to prove that you're not the mess-up that you're convinced they think you are.

That's exhausting. It's depressing. And it's a far cry from God's abundant life.

Rather than trying to prove that you have something to say, you should tell yourself, "God has taught me a lot. He has given me a gift. He knows the people I need to help, and what I say matters. This isn't even about me. It's about them, and it's about Christ working through me."

You can tell you're operating from a place of "not enough" by asking yourself: Where am I trying to prove myself instead of just *being* myself? Where am I forgetting that God's power is in my presence, not my perfection? Where do I need to get out of my head and into God's grace?

Are you facing something intimidating? Silence the inner critic, the distracting chatter, the voices that say, "I knew you'd quit. I knew you'd fail. It was only a matter of time."

Focus your faith. You can do this. God prepared you and trained you for this, and he's with you all the way.

I know we all feel like imposters once in a while. And the inner questions are not always a bad thing—they keep us honest and humble. But if we are more focused on proving we are not frauds than on being our real selves, something needs to change.

I think the apostle Paul dealt with imposter syndrome sometimes, but he knew how to process it. He wrote, "For I am the least of the apostles and do not even deserve to be called an apostle, because I persecuted the church of God. But by the grace of God I am what I am, and his grace to me was not without effect. No, I worked harder than all of them—yet not I, but the grace of God that was with me" (1 Corinthians 15:9–10).

Notice two things here. First, Paul recognized his mistakes in the past, but he didn't spiral into self-hatred. He didn't say, "I can't do anything right. I'm a total failure. I'm a terrible apostle. I don't even know why you guys are reading my letter."

Second, he didn't base his identity on his successes either. He recognized his accomplishments honestly, but he didn't make them the source of his security.

Instead, he focused on God's grace, which is his power at work in each of us. He was saying, "I am what I am by the grace of God. His grace is powerful, and I'm going to walk in courage and confidence—but at the end of the day, I don't have to be perfect. I don't have anything to prove. I can rest in what God accomplished."

Of course, if you're going to believe that you are enough, you have to learn how to silence the voice of comparison. Comparison is a killer. It's a liar. It's a thief. It steals your confidence and joy in who you are by telling you that because you *have* less or *do* less than someone else, you *are* less.

> If you're going to believe that you are enough, you have to learn how to silence the voice of comparison.

My weight-lifting buddy Buck sent Elijah and me a workout the other day. It was ridiculous. If we had tried to do what Buck wanted us to do, it would have ended in injury or vomit or both. So I told Elijah what Buck wanted us to do, and then I told him what we were actually going to do—and it was about half of what Buck had sent over.

Elijah looked at me funny, like maybe we were cheating by cutting the workout in half. I said, "Elijah, don't feel bad. Buck is just built different."

Years ago, I might have felt bad about modifying the routine. Not anymore. I know who I am, and I know who I'm not—and I'm not Buck. There is only one Buck. He's just built different.

So are you.

You were built by God to be exactly who you are. He planned you, and he's proud of you.

Where do you feel like you're not enough? Is it in school, because no matter how hard you try, your grades don't show it? Is it with your friends, because you always feel like the odd one out? Is it when you scroll through social media, because you feel like everyone else is happier than you? In those moments, you need to remind yourself: *I'm built different*. You're not less than, more than, better than, or worse than anyone else.

You're you.

The you that God knew you needed to be.

> You're not less than, more than, better than, or worse than anyone else.
> You're you.
> The you that God knew you needed to be.

ELIJAH

I feel like one of the best gifts God gives us is our voice. The way we talk matters.

Growing up, I'd like to think I was always a pretty intelligent speaker. But as I got older, I started noticing something. The kids around me at school began to dumb down how they talked. Some of them were trying to act cool and nonchalant. Other people were throwing cuss words in between every possible gap in their sentences. And I started wondering—Do I need to change how I talk? Are people going to think I'm weird if I keep speaking like I was raised with some sense?

I can't lie—it was hard not to conform.

And I can't say I did the best job. Heck, I can't even say I've got it all figured out now. None of us do.

But when I think back on how much I dumbed down the way I spoke just to match the people around me, it honestly makes me sad.

Because I believe God puts His light in all of us. And that light is supposed to come out when we speak.

When we dumb that down, I feel like it's one of the most disrespectful things we can do to God.

The older I've gotten, the more I've learned to never downplay the gifts that God has given me. Even when it's hard to be the one who stands out in your friend group, you'll realize no one's really judging you. Honestly, when you let those gifts shine, I feel like people usually respect you more.

So now, I just try to remember to never hold back my real self.

God made me exactly the way I'm supposed to be.

Don't compare yourself to the person who always seems confident or the friend who is always the center of attention. Don't compare your talents or personality to someone else's. You were made to excel in your own way. And honestly, you have no idea what someone else is dealing with behind the scenes. Comparison will steal your joy and make you forget who you really are. Don't fall for it.

Now, if you need to change in some area, God will make that clear. As I said earlier, God fully accepts you today, *and* you can keep becoming the truest version of who he made you to be. Both of those things are true at the same time.

Accepting your Self is not about never changing, but rather about believing you are perfectly loved and accepted right now, and there is nothing you could do to make God love you more. It's about believing that God knows your weaknesses and the challenges you face, and he will show himself strong through them.

> There is nothing you could do to make God love you more.

So accept your Self. Embrace who you are. Love who God made you while you continue to grow into the person he enables you to be. Practice being the version of you that matches God's vision—the true you.

I still can't read Greek like my old professor, and I probably never will. I can't lift weights like Buck, and I don't even want to. I can't wrestle like Helen, but I can sure cheer her on. There are so many things I can't do—but that's okay. I've made peace with it. I am who I am by the perfect, powerful, and permanent grace of God.

And so are you.

NINE

COMING FROM ABUNDANCE

One time when Elijah was really young, he grabbed five napkins at dinner. *Five.* He wasn't handing them out to the family either. I'm talking about one kid...one meal...five napkins.

I hate to admit it, but I freaked out a little. Then I stopped myself. Why was this such a huge issue to me? Shouldn't I be glad he was cleaning his face and hands like a civilized person instead of using his shirt and pants the way he used to?

Why was I losing it over *napkins*?

Suddenly I remembered something. When I was a kid, my dad would always tear paper towels in half at dinner, and he'd say, "You don't need a whole paper towel sheet. Half is enough. Learn how to get by with half."

He grew up very poor, so he was serious about not wasting money. He drilled it into us.

Some of that mindset was healthy—but some was not.

As I watched Elijah go through napkins like he didn't even care that they could run out, I realized something. I'd carried my dad's scarcity mentality into my own adulthood without thinking about it.

And that—right there—was the problem: *I had never thought about it.* I was still looking at life and napkins from a place of lack. Sure, five napkins were overkill for one meal. But I needed to loosen up a little.

Here's my question, though: Are there any areas where *you* are carrying around a scarcity mindset, and you haven't stopped to think about it? Where you've never questioned why you are so afraid, so defensive, so limited?

I'm not talking about how many napkins you use at dinner. I'm talking about the way you see your resources. The way you see your relationships. The way you manage your money. The way you plan your schedule. The way you dream for the future. The way you use your free time.

Do you look at life with a mindset of lack? Or one of abundance?

See, the connection between "Christ is in me" and "I am enough" is meant to be one of abundance. I can't imagine Jesus keeping track of napkins at the Last Supper. He turned a picnic lunch into a meal for a multitude. He wasn't really worried about running out of stuff.

So why am I? Why are you? Why do we so often look at life through the filter of *not enough*?

In her book *The Gifts of Imperfection*, Brené Brown says "never enough" is the way most of us feel about almost everything. And she's right. When I feel anxious or upset, I can usually connect it to a never enough mindset: "I never get enough sleep. I never have enough money. I never have enough time. I never have enough energy."

But if I take that kind of thinking into my day, it's a setup to fail. It's a disaster waiting to happen.

GRAHAM

This trap is something I tend to find myself caught up in a lot. There is always this perfect version of myself that I am chasing. I always think, "If I can just get ___, then I will be content." But every time I get whatever that might be, there is something new that I start to chase. This can happen a lot within my sport, which is wrestling. I see on social media all of these people accomplishing things that I want to and I convince myself that if I just accomplish something like them, then everyone will love me and be proud of me. I spend so much time in the grind trying to get to the next thing that I forget to enjoy the things that are happening now.

For example, my sophomore year, I won my first state title in wrestling. I thought my whole life, and especially the year leading up to it, that if I can just become a state champ, then life will be perfect. After I won, I was content for a little while, but eventually I became focused on winning the next one.

As I've gotten older and more mature, I've learned to enjoy the things that are happening now. I have learned to accept that I'll never be more loved than I am right now by God, so why would it matter how much other people love me? Escaping this trap has brought me so much joy. I have learned to be where

> my feet are and to not get so caught up in who I am going to be in the future.
>
> Being content with where God has me and the abundance he has given me has also helped me to escape the trap of comparing myself to others. I now understand that my journey looks different than everyone else's and God has me exactly where he wants me.

Jesus said he came to give life and life more abundantly. That means the true you can face whatever the day brings from a place of abundance, not lack.

You have to *put on* that mindset, though. You have to tap into the version of you that comes from abundance. If you keep talking about how you never get enough sleep, you'll always feel tired. If you keep complaining about not having enough time, you'll always feel stressed out.

The conversations you have inside your head matter a lot. So make sure that what you're telling yourself about your challenges, worries, and weaknesses lines up with the abundance of God.

> The conversations you have inside your head matter a lot.

Now, if you slept only three hours last night, you probably can't talk yourself into feeling rested. This isn't about denying reality. What I'm saying is, don't make "never enough" the filter you see your life through.

What does coming from abundance look like? It looks like believing every morning that *you have enough time and energy for what God has called you to do today.*

Remembering that truth will keep you from going into the day already defeated. It will help you take some of the pressure off yourself. You don't have to do everything perfectly today. You don't have to get everything done in the next week.

Instead of spiraling into dark thoughts of never enough, talk yourself into an attitude of abundance. "God's grace is enough for me today. I don't need to do everything—I just have to do what God has called me to do today. His abundance is all I need."

On a practical level, how do you come into your day from abundance? Let me give you four ways.

First, make sure you're clear on the *priorities* God has for you.

Jesus said, "Seek first his kingdom and his righteousness, and all these things will be given to you as well" (Matthew 6:33). So if you feel like you aren't enough, start by checking whether you're chasing the right things. Does God really want you to have that car you're working so hard to buy? Do you need to worry so much about impressing people whose opinions won't even matter in the long run? Do you have to meet all your friends' expectations, or do you need to set some boundaries?

Remember, God gives you enough resources for what you're meant to do, so if you don't have enough time or energy, it might not be a resource problem—it might be a priority problem.

> If you don't have enough time or energy, it might not be a resource problem—it might be a priority problem.

Second, you come from abundance when you stay in God's *presence*.

Inviting Jesus into your heart and life means a lot more than just salvation from sins. It means you have his power and presence within you wherever you go and whatever you face. What challenge are you facing today? You have great needs, but you have a greater God, a God who lives in you and flows through you.

Paul said, "I can do all things through Christ who strengthens me" (Philippians 4:13 NKJV). Jesus strengthens *you* so you can face all the things that need your attention. That teacher who seems like he's out to get you. The friend group that ghosted you. The relationship with your dad that seems too broken to heal. The addiction you're ashamed to tell anyone about. The scholarship you desperately need but seems so out of reach.

Whatever the day holds, Christ is always with you. His presence is your strength.

Here's a third way to come from abundance: *proactivity*. Don't just sit back and wait for life to happen. Make progress on what God is showing you. Maybe that means getting a part-time job. Maybe it means sending out college applications. Maybe it means asking a certain person out on a date. Do the thing that you would do if you knew you would be up for the challenge.

Fear will try to paralyze you, but faith in God's abundance will empower you. If you believe God is with you, if you believe he's faithful to his word, if you believe he's given you all you need—then take action. The Bible says that "faith by itself, if it is not accompanied by action, is dead"

(James 2:17). Do what the faith-filled version of you would do because that's the true you.

Finally, coming from abundance means having *patience*. Sometimes you have to work for a long time before you see the result. A mindset of abundance means you trust that God will do the right work, at the right time, the right way. There's no need to panic.

There's another passage in James that says, "Be patient, then, brothers and sisters, until the Lord's coming. See how the farmer waits for the land to yield its valuable crop, patiently waiting for the autumn and spring rains. You too, be patient and stand firm, because the Lord's coming is near" (5:7–8).

I don't know a lot about agriculture, but I do know that not everything you plant will come up at the same time or in the same way. Seeds have their own schedule, and so do God's promises.

A lot of things are beyond your control. Instead of forcing things, often you have to farm them. You have to water them. You have to wait for them.

If you tried to talk to a close friend who is mad at you, but she blew you off yet again, be patient. Don't rise to her level of emotion. Keep loving her and reaching out to her. You'll get through this. Don't force it. Farm it.

If the music you are writing, the sport you are training for, the illness you are facing, or the trauma you are healing from is taking longer than you expected, be patient. Don't force it. Farm it.

Christ is in you, so you are enough. You can come from abundance if you seek God's *priorities*, find peace in his *presence*, be *proactive* by taking practical steps of faith, and stay *patient* for as long as it takes.

What challenge are you facing? In what areas has "never enough" felt like a mantra on repeat in your mind? You don't have to live with a mindset of lack. Quit counting napkins and start counting blessings. Then step into the abundant version of you, the true you.

Whatever you're up against, whatever dark thoughts try to creep into your head, make this the mindset you rest in and stand upon: *Christ is in me. I am enough.*

Confidence in God's presence and your purpose will lead you into action. It will carry you to victory. When you really believe God is with you, you see obstacles as possibilities. You find yourself excited about the future, not just worried about the present.

> When you really believe God is with you, you see obstacles as possibilities.

A focus on possibility is the essence of the next mindset I want to share with you: *With God there's always a way, and by faith I will find it.*

MINDSET (03)

WITH GOD THERE'S ALWAYS A WAY, AND BY FAITH I WILL FIND IT.

ACTION STEP:
FOCUS ON POSSIBILITY.

TEN

FORWARD, NOT FINISHED

My friend Rick Beato runs one of my favorite YouTube channels. Rick tells the best stories about musicians, and he breaks down music concepts so well that every song he talks about instantly becomes your favorite song.

When I first started watching Rick's channel with my son Graham, he had less than fifty thousand subscribers. Today he has over five *million*.

That's impressive. But what makes Rick's story so incredible is that he started the channel when he was fifty-four years old. He joined the social media universe with gray hair and half his life behind him. That doesn't happen every day.

Before Rick started his channel, he had already been a successful music producer for years. But there came a point when things weren't going well in the music business in general, and the work he was doing had started to feel boring. He was discouraged and unsure about the future.

Then he posted a video on Facebook of his son Dylan, who was eight at the time, demonstrating perfect pitch. Now, if you don't know, perfect pitch is the ability to hear a music note and name it by ear, without playing it on an instrument. It's a pretty cool thing to see, especially when an eight-year-old is calling out complex chords like it's the easiest thing in the world. Look up the video and watch it—I promise you, it's worth it.

The video of Dylan went viral. Then someone told Rick, "You should start a YouTube channel."

Rick told me that, at the time, he thought it was a crazy idea. "I looked around, and there was nobody with gray hair like mine on YouTube. I was a producer. I was a music teacher. That's what I did. I was a behind-the-scenes guy. In all my years of producing, I never allowed people to take pictures or videos of me. That's the way I wanted it. I didn't even know how to make videos."

By the time you're fifty-four, you usually have a pretty clear idea of what you can and can't do. But you don't have to be Rick's age to come to these conclusions. Most of us are writing mental summaries of ourselves from the time we're in middle school. "I'm shy. I'm not good at reading. I suck at sports. I can't make friends."

The beautiful thing about Rick is that he was willing to reinvent himself. He decided to start creating videos about anything related to music.

At first, not that many people subscribed. But within a few months, some of the videos started to take off. Slowly but surely, Rick's channel became one of the best places on the internet for music lovers and learners to gather.

Now, Rick has interviewed some of the most famous guitarists of all time, including Dominic Miller, the guitarist for Sting,

Brian May of Queen, Billy Corgan of the Smashing Pumpkins, Peter Frampton, and dozens more. Maybe you've never heard of any of these old rockers, but trust me, they're legends.

So many other YouTubers are younger and grew up in a digital world. How does Rick compete with (and even beat) the best of them? I think it's because—along with his insane work ethic and tremendous talent—he was willing to believe there was more to his story. He was willing to suck at something at first in order to find out what it could be. He was willing to put himself out there in a new way, to see himself differently than he'd seen himself before.

Let me ask you: Are you willing to explore that kind of *what if*? What summary have you written in your head about what you are good at and bad at? What you like and don't like? What you can and can't do? Have you assumed that you are *finished* just because you don't see a way *forward*?

It's one thing to be self-aware and humble. But it's another to roll over and give up, as if your story were over, as if the book of your life were already closed and nothing more could be added. The enemy wants you to think your life is over because you failed a class, or you broke up, or you missed out on an opportunity. But what if your story is just getting started? I promise you—as long as your heart is beating and air is filling your lungs, you're not finished if you're willing to move forward.

This is about openness. "With God there's always a way, and by faith I will find it!" If God wants to reinvent you, will you let him do it? If he wants to heal you, will you let him in? If he wants to fulfill a dream you've given up on, will you let him have his way?

It's easy to *say* yes to these questions, but the real test comes when God sends you an opportunity. Rick had no way of knowing what was ahead of him, and neither do you. You don't have to know—but you do have to be open.

What if I could do this? What if this opportunity is from God? What if this step I'm taking right now is going to change my future? What if it's leading me somewhere God has seen all along?

To you it feels like reinvention, but to God it's a continuation. It's still your story; it's just the next chapter of you. It's the true you.

This mindset points you toward the God of hope and the future he has planned for you. In him, there is always a way—and by faith you'll find it. So when you are tempted to lose hope, don't go back to your old self. Don't settle for old definitions, old limitations, old labels.

Put on your true self. Do the thing that you would do if you believed there was a way, because God is about to open one.

Remember, though, this commitment to possibility is not something you do on your own. Proverbs says, "In their hearts humans plan their course, but the LORD establishes their steps" (16:9). Yes, you should make plans. That's wise, and it's one of the first signs you really have faith. But just because you make your *plans* doesn't mean you make your *way*.

God does that.

You make plans, but God makes paths.

It's easy to get so distracted trying to find your way that you forget about the Waymaker. But he is the source of the help you need. Psalms says, "Where does my help come from? My help comes from the LORD, the Maker of heaven and earth" (121:1–2).

He's a God of possibilities and paths, of redefinitions and reinventions, of wonderful works and unforeseen ways. If he needs a road, he'll make one. If he wants to move a mountain, he'll cast it into the sea. He built the world and he runs the world.

Maybe you can't see very far past graduation, but God sees your entire life. Your days are written in his book, and they are precious to him. Maybe you don't have the family background you wish you had, or the money, or the skills, or the opportunities—but God put you exactly where you need to be. Quit telling yourself you're finished before you've even started. Quit voting yourself off the island before you've even played the game.

> Quit telling yourself you're finished before you've even started.

God runs things, and he will make a way. He doesn't follow human timetables. He doesn't depend on human politics or economy. He doesn't check the weather to see if it's a good time for him to act today. He doesn't ask about your age or height or experience or education. He opens whatever way he wants, whatever way he wants to.

He is God!

So when you need a way made through something that's beyond your ability, put your faith in him. He split the Red Sea for Israel. He made a highway for them through the desert. He led them into the Promised Land. He fed them with manna from heaven and water from a rock.

If he did all that, he can definitely make a way for you. He can make a way for you to succeed in life even though you don't have the connections you wish you had. He can make a way past the coldness and the distance in your family. He can make a way through addiction to a place of peace and self-control. He can make a way through trauma, through betrayal, through abandonment, through abuse.

There's a story in Luke 5 about a paralyzed man with four friends who were trying to get to Jesus because they knew he could heal their friend. There was a problem, though: They couldn't get through the massive crowd that was gathered around the house Jesus was at. So they got creative. They carried him to the roof, broke open a hole, and used ropes to lower their friend down at the feet of Jesus.

When Jesus saw their faith, he forgave the man's sins and healed him. Because these four people had faith, they found a way past an obstacle, and Jesus did a miracle.

I've had moments like that. I've had miracles like that. I'm sure you have too. In fact, I want you to revisit those memories right now. Think of three things God did for you when you didn't see a way forward. I want you to remember them right now, before you move on. Those are moments to celebrate. They are memories to keep at the forefront of your mind when you're going through hard times.

But not every story ends like that. Sometimes the way forward is not what you expected at all. Sometimes it takes you through pain, heartache, or even tragedy. That doesn't mean you didn't have enough faith, though. Persevering through those hard times is actually the greatest proof of your faith.

There's a man in my church named Tom whose story is

an example of this. Tom's son, Riley, loved fishing and had planned to start a fishing club for young people. Then, tragically, he was killed in a car accident. Tom carried out his son's wish and started a fishing group called Riley's Catch. Today, hundreds of kids have come to Christ through the group. The result doesn't take away Tom's pain or lessen his loss. But he found a way forward, and it was beautiful in its own way.

I could list countless others who found a way through impossible pain because they held on to their unbreakable faith. Yes, they walked through a season of grief. Yes, their hearts were wounded. But God, in his perfect time and gentle way, opened a path of healing and peace for them.

Jesus set the example in this. He carried his cross down a road that we call Via Dolorosa—the way of suffering. The night before, he had prayed, "My Father, if it is possible, may this cup be taken from me. Yet not as I will, but as you will" (Matthew 26:39). But God didn't take the cup from Jesus. Instead, he took Jesus to the cross.

So when I say that with God there's always a way, I'm not saying with God there's always a way around pain and heartache and tragedy. I'm saying there is always a way *through* whatever God allows you to experience. The Bible says, "Even though I walk through the darkest valley, I will fear no evil, for you are with me" (Psalm 23:4).

That's why you need the second half of this mindset: "...and by *faith* I will find it." You need faith when things don't go your way and you have to believe that this is actually God's way.

Sometimes God takes the thing away, and sometimes he takes you through the thing. Either way, he will be faithful,

> **Faith enables you to grow through whatever you go through.**

and he'll keep you safe. And along the way, your faith enables you to *grow* through whatever you *go* through.

I remember one video my friend Rick posted that talked about all the failures that led to his success. He went through the failed bands and the cross-country tours. He talked about getting dropped from a major record label. He described building a studio in his house, only to reach a point where he didn't know how he was going to continue to provide for his family. Then, through a random suggestion to start a YouTube channel—and through his willingness to show up with his whole fifty-four-year-old self and do the work—he found a way to make a bigger difference than he ever imagined. Now he interviews his heroes and touches the lives of millions. God made a way for him, but it took faith to find it.

How about you? Is there something in your life that looks finished, but a voice inside you is telling you that it's not over yet? Is God reminding you, "Go forward! You're not finished"? Listen to that voice. That's the voice of the true you calling you to step into who you really are.

Let faith rise up again. In God, there is a way forward. He is all powerful and always faithful. You might not see the way now, but it will be there when you need it.

By faith you will find it, and step by step you'll walk in it.

ELEVEN

NOW MOVE

A while back I was playing tennis with one of my best friends, who is a much better tennis player than I am. Somehow I was winning this particular game. I'm sure he was just as shocked as I was.

But he did something that really got my attention. Under his breath he said, "Just beat him back, one ball at a time."

He was coaching himself. Encouraging himself. Resetting himself. "Just beat him back, one ball at a time."

And that's what he did. I choked, and he won the game, the set, the match. How? By leaving the past behind and just moving forward.

I watched him do it. He let go of the frustration, he ignored the mistakes he had made, and he focused on the task at hand: Winning the next point. And the next one. And so on until he had completely destroyed my already fragile ego.

I don't know about you, but I get stuck in the past a lot. That dumb thing I said yesterday. That moment last night when I snapped at my family. That comment someone made online that I can't stop thinking about. That idea I was so excited about that ended up falling through.

It's easy to let things like that lock us into a doom loop of discouragement. But if we just stand there, stuck in guilt or shame or grief or disappointment, we'll end up losing the game.

A mindset that says, "With God there's always a way, and by faith I will find it," doesn't mean you will never make a mistake or feel discouraged. It doesn't mean you'll never miss what you used to have or be nervous about the future. It means you're willing to leave the past behind and keep pushing forward.

This is often as simple as recognizing that you have a choice. You're not actually stuck in that doom loop. Within you lies the power to reset, to shift, to walk toward a better future.

I had a moment just the other day when I was trying to correct one of my kids about something (not napkins) and it got a little more heated than I intended. Correction: *I* got more heated than I intended. It wasn't terrible: I wasn't cussing or throwing plates around the room or anything like that. But it shifted the energy in the room, and I thought, *Oh, man! Now I ruined the whole morning.*

But then I stopped myself. I thought, *You didn't ruin it. Just shift it.*

After about a minute of working through that incident, we shifted. We recovered, and the rest of the morning was good.

Do you see how practical this is? How immediate? It's a choice you make to keep moving forward, even in the smallest things you say and do.

That's how you win at life. One positive thought at a time. One faith-filled prayer at a time. One right choice at a time. One kind word at a time. Sometimes we imagine that breaking out of a bad mood, a bad day, or a bad situation is a major event—but often it's as simple as doing the next right thing.

So ask yourself: "What does moving forward look like for me, right now? What is the next thing, the new thing, the *now* thing that I need to do? The next word I speak will be positive. The next question I ask will be curious, not cynical. The next move I make will be full of energy."

> What does moving forward look like for me, right now? What is the next thing, the new thing, the *now* thing that I need to do?

I don't mean to say this is always easy. Life is a lot more complicated than a tennis match. It's one thing to tell yourself to put the past behind you and look forward, but it's another to *do* the next right thing. That takes all your focus and energy. Then you do it again. And again.

It's not easy.

But it is possible.

You can beat the enemy back, one ball at a time.

When Israel reached the border of the Promised Land, while they were in a place called the plains of Moab, God took Moses to the top of a mountain and showed him the land from a distance. The Bible says that, after that, Moses died at the age of one hundred and twenty, and God buried him in a place that nobody knew.

Can you imagine how Israel must have felt as they waited at the foot of that mountain? Moses had already told them God wasn't going to let him lead them into the Promised Land, but I'll bet they still had a hard time believing he wasn't returning.

Israel needed Moses—or so they thought. He had been their leader for forty years. He had given them food from heaven and water from a rock. He was the one who spoke to God on their behalf when they had sinned. He was the one they looked to for direction. There was only one Moses.

So I'm going to speculate that while they were mourning for Moses, they were also looking for him. I bet they were mobilizing search parties and holding prayer meetings, hoping to see him walk back down the mountain.

The Bible says, "The Israelites grieved for Moses in the plains of Moab for thirty days, until the time of weeping and mourning was over" (Deuteronomy 34:8). The normal time for grieving in that culture was a week, but Moses was special. He was legendary. So Israel took a whole month to mourn him.

At some point, though, they had to accept the fact that Moses wasn't coming back. Moses was no more.

What now? What next?

It was a moment of decision. The Promised Land was on the horizon. It was in their future, and they were looking forward to it. But in order to step into what was next, they had to leave something behind.

That's not easy. It wasn't easy for them, and it's not easy for us. It takes time in seasons of change to let go of what feels so comfortable, so familiar, so safe. But holding on to those things for too long will keep us from fully stepping into our future.

Change can be hard. It can feel sad sometimes because

you're leaving some things behind. There are better things ahead, though. That's what you need to remember. God knows about them, but you don't—not yet.

Uncomfortable seasons remind me of those social media posts that say "Wait for it" or "Wait till the end" because most people's attention spans are about two seconds long, and if they swipe or scroll, they'll miss the good part of the video. "Wait for it" means wait and watch what happens, because the best part is coming.

In the same way, the good part of your life is coming. Don't give up on your current situation too quickly. Don't swipe or scroll past it. Don't call it unimportant, boring, bad, pointless, a waste of time, a loss. Something is about to happen that you don't see coming.

Wait for it.

There's so much more to your story. Don't close your heart. Don't close your mind. Don't stop praying. Don't stop believing.

In your life, some of the characters are going to exit. Some of your friends are going to leave. Some of your circles might change. There will be seasons when you feel like you're losing or like the pain will never go away, but don't let that convince you it will always be that way. Maybe God had to remove or change some things in order to make room for what is coming next. Don't think the death of Moses is the end of a dream.

> Maybe God had to remove or change some things in order to make room for what is coming next.

Holly was talking to me the other day about how someone who had been her friend for nearly twenty years seemed to be shutting her out of their life, almost overnight. Holly was sad and hurt because a relationship she really cared about was ending.

As we talked, we realized something: That friendship wasn't a waste. It wasn't a failure. It had been a gift for almost twenty years. Now, instead of focusing on the loss, she needed to focus on new relationships that were opening up. As she listed the new friends God had been sending her recently, her perspective changed. That didn't mean the old friendship was fake or unimportant—but it was time to accept the change and move forward.

If you're going through change or loss right now, the pain is real and the grief is valid. But if God allowed something to be taken away from you, he's probably also adding something to you. Can you see it? Can you wait for it? Can you believe it?

Deuteronomy says that Israel grieved until "the time of weeping and mourning was over." They spent a month mourning Moses in Moab. Try saying that five times in a row. A *m*onth *m*ourning *M*oses in *M*oab.

It's a lot of *mo*'s. And they all ended at once.

"No Mo" is how I think of it. No more Moses. No more mourning a past that will never exist again. No more camping out in Moab hoping for the good old days to return. *No Mo.* The time had come to move forward into the promise of God.

Notice it doesn't say the *feeling* of mourning was over. But the *time* for mourning was over. That wasn't meant to be cruel. God wasn't saying, "It's over. Get over it. Stop crying. Quit whining. Grow up." And I'm not saying that either. They took a month to mourn because emotions matter.

But eventually, at the right time, mourning needed to give way to movement. They had to go from *No Mo* to *Now Move*.

Your walk with God includes feelings, but your faith is a lot bigger than feelings. Sometimes you have to move forward even when you're still feeling something from the past. You have to move forward even when it still doesn't make sense. You have to move forward when you still have unanswered questions. You have to move forward when you still feel hurt by their actions. You have to move forward when you still feel rejected, overlooked, or misunderstood.

> Sometimes you have to move forward even when you're still feeling something from the past.

Are you in a No Mo season right now? Is it your time to move forward even though you're mourning and missing something you're leaving behind? Have you been holding on to a past that God is asking you to let go of so you can move forward in peace? Jesus told one of his disciples, "Follow me, and let the dead bury their own dead" (Matthew 8:22). In other words, don't let what is dead stop you from living.

Maybe it's time to move out of Moab, to stop looking for a Moses who isn't coming back. To stop reliving a season of your life that was awesome but is over now. To quit waiting for someone to apologize for hurting you. To stop longing for a romance that didn't work out. To accept your parents' divorce and love them both even though they made a lot of mistakes. To believe that there is joy on the other side of loss.

You've mourned long enough; now it's time to move forward.

That "month of mourning" is figurative, by the way. If you dropped your phone and broke the screen, you shouldn't need a literal month to grieve. If you lost a loved one, though, you might never "get over" it—and I'm not saying you need to. You'll carry the loss forever, although it won't always hurt as badly as it does now. But you can still move forward when the time is right.

I love the Bible verse that says, "Weeping may stay for the night, but rejoicing comes in the morning" (Psalm 30:5). We're going forward with our tearstained faces, forward with our unanswered questions, forward with our unfinished faith—but forward.

The story doesn't end with the death of Moses, as I said. Right after the mourning period is over, Deuteronomy 34 says, "Now Joshua son of Nun was filled with the spirit of wisdom because Moses had laid his hands on him" (verse 9).

Notice the first two words: "Now Joshua."

God took them from No Mo to Now Joshua. For every No Mo in your life, there is a Now Joshua that God has been developing. In other words, when you see an ending, God is already making a new opening. Where you see no way, God says, "Now, watch me make a way."

You're not finished; you're moving forward. Something is over, but something else is beginning. And what happens next depends on how you respond. Paul wrote, "Forgetting what is behind and straining toward what is ahead, I press on toward the goal to win the prize for which God has called me heavenward in Christ Jesus" (Philippians 3:13–14).

What do you need to leave behind so you can move

forward? What do you need to mourn for a season, then leave behind in God's hands?

You can miss what you've lost *and* move into what's ahead. You can be upset that a friendship ended and still trust that God is bringing new people into your life. You can miss the town you lived in for a while and be open to the new opportunities in the city God moved your family to. You can be grateful for what brought you to this point *and* choose to leave those things behind and move forward. Don't miss out on what's next (Joshua) because you're stuck missing what was (Moses).

What is your "Now Joshua"? What doors are opening? What people are coming into your life? What faith is stirring in your heart? What challenges are waiting ahead? What calling has God awakened in your heart?

What is the new thing, the now thing, the next thing that God is doing in you?

Now move.

TWELVE

WEASEL-FREE MENTALITY

I love the book *The Artist's Way* by Julia Cameron. One of the things she writes about is the internal "censor" or the voice that sabotages your creativity. She says your censor is the part of yourself that criticizes you and makes fun of you when you start to create. It's the voice that says your work is mediocre and you have no business doing this.

I think her point applies to more than just creativity. I think the same dynamic exists in our walk with Jesus as we become who he has called us to be. Walking in the mindset "With God there's always a way, and by faith I will find it" means learning to silence the inner voice that comes after your creativity, your confidence, and your courage.

Maybe you've experienced this. Maybe you have an internal voice that tries to keep you locked into the old you—the fearful, self-critical, defensive you—instead of allowing you to explore, try new things, and find out what you're capable of doing. That's the *opposite* of a mindset that focuses on possibility.

Julia Cameron suggests finding a cartoon image that represents the inner doubt—what she calls the "censor"—and putting it somewhere you can see it when you are trying to create. She says, "Just making the Censor into the nasty, clever little character that it is begins to pry loose some of its power over you and your creativity."*

In other words, when you realize the censor doesn't get to tell you who you really are, you break free from its power. You find freedom.

When I read that, I decided that I would make my censor a weasel. Why? First, the image fits. Weasels are creepy-looking and destructive. They sneak into gardens and steal the fruit before it's ready to harvest. I think that's the perfect metaphor not only for things that block creativity but also for things that sabotage spiritual growth.

When something is growing, it needs to be nurtured, but when we criticize and judge it, we interrupt the process. We spoil the fruit before it has a chance to grow into what it could be.

The second reason I picked a weasel is because of a sermon I preached one time about weasels. You might not have known that the Bible talks about weasels. I didn't either, until I came across it in Leviticus. Let me give you a quick recap of that sermon because it connects to the mindset we're looking at here.

Leviticus says that the weasel was an unclean animal for the Israelites. That meant they couldn't eat it—which is hard

---

* Julia Cameron, *The Artist's Way: A Spiritual Path to Higher Creativity* (New York: Penguin Group, 2002). Kindle edition (loc. 511).

to imagine doing in the first place, but I guess God had to make it clear because some people will eat anything.

It also meant that if a weasel died, it would contaminate anything it touched, such as a vessel or clothing. That was the law for all dead animals. The item had to be purified or thrown out.

But there was an exception to the dead-animal rule. The Bible says, "If a carcass falls on any seeds that are to be planted, they remain clean" (11:37).

When I saw that verse hidden in Leviticus, I realized it was a powerful metaphor. Seeds represent possibility. They represent growth and fruit. Sometimes, though, it can seem like a weasel came into your life and dropped dead on top of your seed. It tried to contaminate your dreams, your confidence, your joy, your relationships.

Have you ever felt like there was a dead weasel lying on the seed of your hope? Maybe the weasel was an unmet expectation. A bad doctor's report. A failing grade. A rejection. You thought something had potential—and then it seemed to die.

But it's not the *potential* that died. The dream or idea or calling is still there, but there's a weasel on it. You're listening to a censor, a voice, a fear, or a threat that wants you to give up on what God gave you.

I've got good news for you. The seed is still clean. The seed still has life in it. The dream you had can still come true. The future you thought God had for you is still possible. Even if that weasel has tried to steal what God put there, even if it seems like something died right on top of your dreams, it doesn't kill the seed. The devil can't take from you what God has put in you.

Seeds are powerful, and their power is in their potential. What seems like a small thing—an idea, a thought, a sketch you made in your notebook, an encouraging text you wrote to a friend, a smile at the kid you know has been hurting—is the seed of something that can hold more potential than you may currently see.

You know what is crazy? Sometimes it seems like the enemy believes in our potential more than we do. That's why he sends those little weasels. Weasels of worry. Weasels of inferiority. Weasels that tell you this isn't worth it or you're not worth it. Weasels that say, "This isn't working. It doesn't even matter. That's so stupid. Who do you even think you are to attempt that?" Weasels that die on your seed and make you think the seed itself is dead.

But seeds never die. And weasels always lie.

Don't listen to weasels. Don't listen to the lies that try to convince you that there is nothing good inside you. You have to protect your mind, your emotions, and your decisions from lies that interrupt what is still growing. You have to guard that vulnerable place where you nurture what God is speaking, or even what you think he *might* be speaking.

> Don't listen to the lies that try to convince you that there is nothing good inside you.

The day I named my inner critic the Weasel, I wrote down on a piece of paper, "Weasel-free since 2023." I declared it over my heart. I even ordered two customized aluminum signs, one for me and one for Elijah, to hang up in the places we usually create, that say, WEASEL-FREE SINCE 2023. They have an image of a weasel with a big line through it. I'm either the most creative dad ever or the cheesiest, depending on your taste in home decor.

That sign makes me smile every time I see it. It reminds me that my imagination belongs to God, that my heart is his garden.

On the other hand, sometimes I look at it and think, *That's pretty silly. Nobody knows what that means. What kind of grown man makes signs that say weasel-free?*

Do you see the irony there? The sign is meant to critique my self-critical nature so I can break free from it, but then I start criticizing my critique of my self-criticism. (And right now I'm criticizing *that*.)

Welcome to weasel world. Welcome to my tormented mind. I'm tormented, but I'm trying.

Keeping a heart weasel-free is hard work, so whenever I have an idea and I hear weasel words, I say—usually silently but sometimes out loud—"Get off my seed, weasel! I know it's just an idea. That's all it's supposed to be. It's just a seed. I don't have to decide what to do with it yet. Maybe I'll forget about it. Maybe I'll hang it on my wall. Maybe I'll tattoo it on my arm. Maybe I'll preach about it. I don't have to judge it yet. I can just enjoy it while it grows."

I want *you* to learn how to enjoy things as they grow. Some of the things that God speaks to you aren't meant to become a reality in this stage of your life. That's okay—you've got a lifetime to let those seeds grow. Don't let the weasel destroy the potential just because you don't see your dreams come true in the next two years.

By the way, other people can be censors too, sometimes without even trying. A random comment like "Wow, that's kind of weird" can become a weasel that gets into our thought processes and steals our uniqueness. Remember, people speak from their own perspectives and experiences. Don't let anyone else's limitation become your insecurity.

> Don't let anyone else's limitation become your insecurity.

At the same time, don't be a weasel to other people either. When we're hypercritical of other people's ideas, when we ignore someone's contribution, or when we interrupt what someone else is sharing with an idea we think is better, we don't give their seed space to grow. We're being weasels.

One time, Paul wrote, "I care very little if I am judged by you or by any human court; indeed, I do not even judge myself. My conscience is clear, but that does not make me innocent. It is the Lord who judges me" (1 Corinthians 4:3–4).

Paul was talking about people who criticized him. He wasn't saying he never evaluated his way of life—he had a clear conscience, so obviously he was doing his best. Instead, he was saying he didn't let weasels prematurely interrupt the process. He wasn't going to second-guess everything, defend everything, or attach a disclaimer to everything, just to avoid the possibility of being criticized.

He added, "Therefore judge nothing before the appointed time; wait until the Lord comes. He will bring to light what is hidden in darkness and will expose the motives of the heart. At that time each will receive their praise from God" (verse 5). God is the judge. He's the only one qualified to know the true nature of anything.

I especially love the last phrase there. When God exposes

the motives of the heart, we will receive *praise*. That's hard for me to believe. I tend to think that God is going to expose my pride, or my selfishness, or my insecurity, or my short temper.

That's not the nature of God, though. He creates a safe space for you to grow and thrive. He's not like that teacher or family member who delights in pointing out your mistakes. He's not micromanaging you. He's not censoring your creativity. He's not making fun of your mess-ups.

He's looking for reasons to praise you. And he finds them everywhere.

I want to respect and protect the living seeds God sends me. I'm learning to give myself permission to process my ideas rather than giving up on them because of a criticism, a doubt, or a weird comment from someone.

> God's not making fun of your mess-ups. He's looking for reasons to praise you. And he finds them everywhere.

That means I'm going to scribble ideas down when I have them, even if they seem silly. I'm going to sing ideas for songs into my phone so I don't forget them. I'm going to share encouraging thoughts with a friend, even if I don't express myself perfectly. I'm going to show up for my friends and family, even if I don't have it all together when I do. I'm going to lean into opportunities to help people, knowing that they will be messy and imperfect.

As for me and my house, we will be weasel-free. I want my kids to know it's okay to create something just for the joy of creating it. If it's not hurting anybody, and if they're not making meth, go ahead! Be creative. Make something, say something, do something. I want to be the kind of person who doesn't mock what somebody else is working on or working through, but rather gives them space to see what their seed can be.

How about you? What weasels do you need to silence? What seeds do you need to plant? What dreams do you need to focus on in this season of your life? What small steps can you take today in order to plant the seeds of what you want to walk into tomorrow?

Remember, with God there is always a way, and by *faith* you will find it—not by self-doubt or self-ridicule. Not by asking for the opinion of weasels. Not by letting your inner censor bully you into blandness. Not by sitting on seeds that are meant to be planted. You find your way forward by ignoring the inner critic and sowing your seeds in faith.

> You never know what the seed will produce until you plant it.

You never know what the seed will produce until you plant it, and you can't plant it until you get the weasel off it. Declare your heart weasel-free and see what your seed can be.

THIRTEEN

WHAT IF THIS SUCCEEDS?

The other day I came across a demo version of a song I had written a long time ago. I played it for Holly. It was about ten years old, and it was cringey, to say the least. I laughed out loud as we listened because I couldn't believe we'd thought it was worth recording at the time.

Holly looked confused and a little annoyed. Finally, she asked, "Why are you playing this?" It was her polite way of begging me to turn it off.

But then, about two minutes in, we came to one line that she recognized, and her expression changed. You see, even though most of that song ended up on the cutting room floor, there were a few lines that went on to become part of another song that we still sing today, years later. In fact, it's one of the most well-loved songs our church has ever released. It turned out that even in a bad song, there were good lines.

I remember all the writing sessions around that first track. We tried time after time to make it work, to force it to take shape. And every time, we failed. It was frustrating. But eventually, those failed attempts produced a beautiful thing that continues to encourage people and point them to God. Buried within something bad were the seeds of something special.

Why do I share this? Because this is true in many areas of our lives. Often the seed of tomorrow's success is hidden within today's failure.

Great things rarely come easily. They hardly ever happen on the first try. That's the unsexy truth of the creative process, and it's the reality of life in general. It's true whether you're trying to learn a sport, take up a hobby, record an album, write a children's book, become an influencer, start a business, invent new technology, or do anything else that stretches you beyond your current capacity.

Remember, the true-you mentality says, "With God there's always a way, and by faith I will find it." Exploring possibilities and knocking on doors can feel frustrating, but that doesn't mean you're doing it wrong. You're trying something new. You're building something step by step.

At first, that thing you are doing—like the song I played for Holly—might seem to suck. You might say, "Why am I here? Why am I doing this? What is the point of all this? This is embarrassing."

> Maybe what you think sucks is actually a seed. Maybe your future will be found in your frustration and your failures.

But maybe what you think sucks is actually a seed. Maybe your future will be found in your frustration and your failures. Maybe your first drafts, your first steps, your first attempts will set something in motion that God will make beautiful in his time.

Instead of getting depressed over the mistakes along the way, why not focus on the possibilities ahead? Why not dream about what could happen? Imagine the people you could impact. Imagine the things you could create. Imagine the life you could enjoy.

I came across a scripture several years ago that talks about this, and I've gotten obsessed with it. I find it to be mysterious, and yet in its mystery, it's clarifying.

"Sow your seed in the morning, and at evening let your hands not be idle, for you do not know which will succeed, whether this or that, or whether both will do equally well" (Ecclesiastes 11:6).

Using agriculture as an illustration, Solomon was telling us to try different things, even though we don't know if they'll work or not. It's good advice because many of us are too easily intimidated by this nagging, fear-inducing question: *What if it fails?*

Someone once suggested to me, "Why don't you flip the question? Say to yourself, *What if it works?*"

It sounds simple, but making that switch changes everything. And that's exactly what Solomon is saying in this verse. "Flip the question! Don't just sit around wondering if your ideas might work or not. Try this one. Try that one too. Because one idea might succeed, or the other, or both of them—but you won't know until you try."

The old you might have said, "What if this crashes and burns? I'd better not even try. Or if I do try, I'm going to aim low. I'm going to expect the worst. I'm going to quit at the first sign of resistance." That version of you might have made excuses and written a resignation speech before failure had even happened. "This probably won't work. I doubt I'll succeed. I'm going to try, but I'm not getting my hopes up."

But that's not the you who God sees. That's not the knew you—the true you.

Why not aim high and risk temporary disappointment, rather than aiming low and guaranteeing a life filled with *what if*s? Instead of predicting your own failure, say, "What if this succeeds beyond my wildest dreams? What if this turns into something I love? What if God plans to take this to places I never expected?"

You're carrying something: a gift, a talent, an idea, a mission, a purpose, a calling. You have to sow your seed so that it has a chance to succeed. You have to step out and try, or you'll never find out what's inside.

> You have to step out and try, or you'll never find out what's inside.

But what if it sucks? It's a fear we all face. So let me be honest with you: *It will suck*. At least for a while. Everything goes through a stage when it's not very good.

In writing, it's called a rough draft. In sports, it's called a drill. In film, it's called a storyboard. In art, it's called a sketch. In technology, it's called a minimum viable product.

It's not pretty. It's not polished. It's a bare-bones version of something that will exist, but a few bugs have to be worked out first. That will take time, and it will go through a lot of iterations along the way.

You have to go through each stage of growth or you'll never get to where God is taking you. But if you're so afraid of looking stupid or making mistakes that you aren't willing to put an imperfect version of yourself out there and fix the flaws that appear along the way, you'll fail by default.

> ## ABBEY
>
> There have been many opportunities in my life that I gave up because I was afraid of looking stupid. But everything in this chapter is so true. If you never fail, you will never grow, and that's something that I've found to be very helpful in my life. Looking back, there have been many auditions and tryouts that I went into so afraid, but then I made the team or got the role I wanted. If I would have clung to my fear so tightly and not tried, I would have missed out on many opportunities.
>
> The beautiful part is that whether you fail or not, the Lord is with you. You can always try again, practice, train, improve, and grow. God gave you strength so you can do these things. But I find it helpful to remember that if you guard yourself from the possibility of looking stupid, you simultaneously rob yourself of the opportunity to succeed. It's better to go in with the Lord and fail—and then grow—than to never even try.

I was in a meeting recently, and someone made a statement that stuck with me. She said, "I'm going to dare to suck right now."

I loved that phrase. She was giving herself permission to be imperfect as we discussed the ideas that were on the table. Permission to try, to explore, to learn, to grow. Permission to make a first-draft fool of herself.

The word "dare" was a good term because real risk is involved, so real courage is needed. When you try new things, you're signing up for a messy process. You might fail spectacularly. You might get laughed at. You might have to apologize. You might lose some followers or waste some time.

Get used to that.

It's part of growth, and it's part of being human. Make peace with your imperfections because perfection is impossible and overrated anyway—but *becoming a fuller version of you* is beautiful.

> **Perfection is impossible and overrated anyway—but *becoming a fuller version of you* is beautiful.**

Even if what you try is really bad at first, you might find some seeds in it. You'll get through the initial stage and say, "Well, all of *that* was bad, but *this* right here is good."

I'm a perfectionist by nature, so I have to continually talk myself through this principle I'm sharing right now. Working on the same song in multiple writing sessions only to end up throwing it out was frustrating, not fun. It made me feel like a fake and a failure. In the moment anyway. But when I hear the song that came from it, I don't think about the pain of the process. I don't remember the suffering in the sowing.

What I feel is the joy of harvest.

Psalms says, "Those who sow with tears will reap with songs of joy. Those who go out weeping, carrying seed to sow, will return with songs of joy, carrying sheaves with them" (126:5–6). A focus on possibility means that you keep your eyes on the hope set before you, not on every little mistake you make along the way.

This isn't denial; it's expectation. It's faith. It's knowing that in God you will find a way forward. It might take a while, and you might have a few false starts and run into a few dead ends, but that's okay. You have to go through all that to get to the benefit on the other side.

One thing I have grown to love—very unexpectedly—is cold plunging. A friend of mine got me to try it a few years ago. In case you've never heard of this voluntary form of self-torture, a cold plunge is when you immerse yourself in ice water for a short time because it's supposed to promote blood circulation, reduce inflammation, and improve mental alertness.

The first time I did it, I stayed in the water for exactly the one minute we had agreed on, then I jumped out and ran to the nearest available sauna. Now, I have to force myself to get out of a cold plunge after ten minutes. I learned this the hard way after staying in a little too long one time and being unable to feel my toes or even walk for fifteen minutes. I'm apparently a little bit of an extremist.

When you first get in that ice-cold water, all you're thinking is, *Why did I voluntarily do this to myself? I'm freezing.* For the first forty-five seconds, that's what fills your mind. *I'm an idiot. I never should have watched that interview with Wim Hof, the Iceman. I want to die right now.*

Then you start to settle. You shiver, but you settle. And to me, it feels really good afterward. Going through the discomfort gets me to a place where I get the benefits.

When it comes to stepping into new things, I think a lot of us never get to the settling because we are afraid of the shivering. We don't plant the seeds because we don't dare to suck.

GRAHAM

I feel like I tend to do this with a lot of things in my life. I let myself get so worked up with fear when I'm starting new things that it becomes really hard to settle. For example, earlier this year, some of my best friends and I started a Bible study. We met on Sunday nights at my house. I remember the first couple of times we did it, only one extra person showed up. I remember thinking, *This was a bad idea. This is so embarrassing. Maybe we are doing something wrong.*

But then around the third or fourth week, we started inviting more friends and having more people show up. After a couple more weeks, we started to have about eight people show up. Now, we have over 400 people coming every Sunday, and it has been one of the best things I've ever been a part of. We have built an awesome community, and it has helped a lot of people grow in their faith.

But it almost didn't happen because I was afraid of the shivering. We were so close to giving up after the first few weeks, but because we pushed through, we have something great.

> This is something I want to apply to every area of my life—trusting God even when I'm shivering. This means that when times get hard, I trust that there is settling on the other side.

I get it. I do the same thing sometimes because the uncertainty of not knowing what will happen is scary. What if it doesn't work? What if they don't like it? What if they reject it?

Well...what if? Play the thought out. Will they *really* remember your failure forever? Will your reputation be ruined beyond repair? I mean, what's the worst thing that could happen?

I'm not saying that the quality of your work doesn't matter. I'm just saying that messing up isn't as big of a deal as the enemy wants you to think. Most people are too busy dealing with their own battles and thinking about their own needs to spend a lot of energy judging you for yours. Plus, many of them are better at showing compassion and mercy to you than you are.

And so is God.

God is a safe place for you to try and fail. If you sink when you try walking on water, Jesus will bring you back to the boat. Not only that, but he'll help you grow through the process, just like he did for Peter. Remember, it was *after* Jesus had stilled the storm that Peter and all the disciples realized, "You really are the Son of God." That light bulb moment happened

> God is a safe place for you to try and fail.

because of Peter's failure. His willingness to try and fail led to a powerful moment of growth.

So here's the principle: God shows up when you slip up.

A lot of us want to live perfect lives, but how can you expect God to show up if you aren't willing to slip up? The cycle of godly success is this: You step up, you slip up, and God shows up. Then you step up again, you slip up again, and God shows up again. And through it all, you grow into the person God knew you would be.

To keep growing and keep sowing, you need to let go of your need for certainty. You need to be okay with not knowing whether something will work or not. If you're sowing enough seeds, some of them will bear fruit. Maybe all of them will. But you won't know if you don't sow.

You should always be sowing something now so you'll have something to reap later. If it doesn't work out, take the seed from the failure and sow it back into the soil of your faith. Give God the mistakes of today and ask him to make them wisdom for your future. And if it does work out, if you do succeed, sow your successes back in by giving praise to God. Turn it into gratitude.

Whatever point of the cycle you're in right now—whether it's the dream, the disappointment, or the wonderful stage called delivery—keep sowing. Keep going. Keep pressing. Use the momentum.

You might deal with some doubts along the way. The weasel may try to tell you that you look stupid, that you're not helping anybody, that you don't know what you're doing. You might hear a voice whisper in your head, "What if this fails?"

Flip the question and whisper back, "But what if it *succeeds*? I'm not stopping. I'm not idle. I'm focusing on possibilities, and I'm looking forward to what God has for me. With God there is always a way, and by faith I will find it."

I love how this mindset starts and ends with God, not just with us. *He* makes the difference. *He* makes us strong. *He* makes a way. God's faithfulness is always the foundation of our faith.

That matters a lot because when life gets hard, it's easy to feel like you have to face everything on your own, like you're trying to navigate a dark forest and all you have is an iPhone flashlight. You can feel overwhelmed by the pressure of it all, scared that if you fail, you'll let everybody down.

You might even feel like you're letting *God* down. I know I do sometimes. I can project my own insecurities onto God, and I start to wonder if maybe I'm on his last nerve, and he's running out of patience with me.

That's why I love this next mindset so much. Don't tell the other mindsets, but I think it's my favorite. It goes like this: *God is not against me, but he's in it with me, working through me, fighting for me.*

> *God is not against me, but he's in it with me, working through me, fighting for me.*

MINDSET (04)

GOD IS NOT AGAINST ME, BUT HE'S IN IT WITH ME, WORKING THROUGH ME, FIGHTING FOR ME.

**ACTION STEP:
WALK IN CONFIDENCE.**

FOURTEEN

THAT LIZARD IS LOUD

My daughter, Abbey, learned to swim underwater when she was seven. She wanted to show her brothers she could cross the pool in one breath—mostly because they couldn't cross it underwater until they were maybe ten. When you're the youngest, little wins matter.

The problem was she had never done it before. So I told her, "All right. We can do this. Just remember, the lizard brain is going to be telling you that you can't do it. But the lizard is lying."

She said, "Wait. There's a lizard in my brain?"

I said, "No, no. It's just that the human brain..." And then I tried to explain to a seven-year-old about the survival part of our brain, the fight-or-flight part that kicks in when we are in an emergency. I told her some people call this the lizard brain.

Now, between the weasel-free mentality we talked about earlier and the lizard brain, you might think I have a strange obsession with critters. I don't. I just like metaphors. And by the way, the science behind the lizard brain theory has been debunked now. I'm a pastor, though, not a psychologist, and at the time, "lizard brain" was a pretty good label for a little girl to understand irrational fear. Since she was seven, she believed me, which is what little kids do. Now she's fourteen years old, and not quite as easily convinced of my scientific explanations. But that's another topic.

Anyway, I told her, "Don't listen to the lizard. You're going to go under the water, and you're going to think you're about to die, but you're not going to die. Just don't listen to the lizard."

She went underwater, swam clear to the other end, and came up gasping but smiling. She was so proud.

I yelled, "Amazing! You did it! How did you feel?"

She said, "Man, that lizard is loud!"

I asked, "What did you say to him?"

She yelled back, "I told him, 'Shut up, lizard! I'm doing this.'"

I loved that response. I use it myself sometimes now: "Shut up, worry! Shut up, insecurity! I'm doing this. I'm moving forward, and you can't stop me."

Are there any areas of your life where you've been listening to the lizard? Where fear has started to take on a voice of its own, and it's telling you that you're going down, you're about to drown, you'll never make it to the other side? Remember, the lizard is a liar.

A lizard brain is the old version you. The true you says, "Shut up, fear. I'm doing this! I'm going to make it. I'm going to get out of this hole I'm in. I'm going to reach the goal I set.

I'm going to make a difference in the world. I'm taking my thoughts back. I'm getting my confidence back."

I'm sure you've noticed that your mind can escalate things quickly. In a split second, your emotions can paint a worst-case picture of the future and take your thoughts to a very dark place. Then you start shrinking back from things that haven't even happened yet because you're imagining forty-seven hypothetically horrible scenarios.

Sometimes that's your brain helping you be smart about danger—but other times it's just the lizard lying to you again. You have to learn what the lizard voice sounds like and tell it to shut up, because it's not the voice of God and it doesn't represent what he thinks about you.

So how do you overcome these thoughts of fear, failure, and worst-case scenarios? First, recognize the lizard voice for what it is: your fight-or-flight instinct spiraling out of control. Then, give your mind something healthier to hold on to.

That's where this mindset comes in.

Earlier, I called it my favorite mindset. It holds a lot of personal meaning for me. Say it out loud, if you can:

God is not against me, but he's in it with me, working through me, fighting for me.

That's what your mind needs to hold on to when the lizard starts lizarding. You have to trust that God wants to work with you. If you don't, how could you possibly handle the pressures of the day, the semester, the year? How could you graduate from school or get a college degree or build a future? How could you press forward through all that uncertainty if you don't believe God is with you and for you?

I love every part of this affirmation. "God is not against me" means that he's not out to get me. He's not mad at me for my mistakes. He's not frustrated with my failure.

"He's in it with me" means we're doing this together. He's not going to abandon me. He's close to me no matter what I'm going through.

"Working through me" means the power comes from him, but I have a part to play. I do what I do by the strength of God at work in me.

And the last phrase, "Fighting for me," means that at the end of the day, the battle belongs to the Lord. God has my back. No one can curse what God has blessed. He's a defender of the weak, and he's fighting on my behalf.

God is not against me, but he's in it with me, working through me, fighting for me. Repeat it to yourself. It's easy to remember, and easy is what you need when the lizard gets loud.

ABBEY

This mindset is so comforting to me as I think about Jesus being not only our closest friend, but our truest friend. When I was little, we sang a song in children's ministry called "Jesus Is My Best Friend." It basically repeats that line over and over. I feel like this mindset is a grown-up version of that, and it is just as helpful. Every messed-up friendship you've been through where you were abandoned or left out cannot even remotely compare to the friendship you have with Jesus, and that's why this mindset is so important.

> This chapter reminds me that Jesus is unlike any friend you've ever had. He has no intention of leaving or forsaking you. He's like one of those friends you look up to and want to be more like, but he's the PERFECT example, and he is in this with you every step of the way.
>
> I think it's such an important reminder that Jesus really is in it with you, and there's nothing you could do that would make him leave your side. There have been countless times where I have been in situations that should have caused me to freak out, but instead I felt the presence of my best friend, Jesus.
>
> He is with you every step of the way. He is planning to HELP you, not leave you!

The story of Gideon in Judges 6 is a good example of a lizard-level reaction. When the story opens, Gideon is in a winepress, and he's busy separating wheat from the stalks. That was a weird place to work, but he was hiding his harvest from the army of Midian, an enemy nation who had been oppressing Israel for years.

A winepress was a hidden place. A low place. A small, closed-in space. I wonder, how often do we hide what God has given us in a small place? Inside a closed-in, limited way of thinking?

When we get scared, we tend to shrink ourselves. We start running from stuff and hiding from stuff, even if nothing is chasing us, and even when God has made us strong enough for the challenge at hand.

I've done that before. You probably have too. Shrinking feels safer, but it's not. Gideon was trying to keep his wheat from the Midianites, but there was no guarantee he was safe down there either. And while he was trying to protect the little he had, the entire land was under attack.

> Shrinking feels safer, but it's not.

He was in survival mode, in fight-or-flight mode. But that's meant to be a temporary setting, not a permanent condition. Now, there will be times when all your energy has to go to survival. Maybe your mom is in the hospital and you're carrying the pressures of school, home, and fear of the future. Maybe you just moved to a new city and every day feels like you're auditioning for a new friend group, and the fear of rejection is overwhelming. In those moments, stress is understandable. Show yourself compassion, and lean on God's grace.

But *staying* in survival mode? *Living* in survival mode? Shrinking yourself and hiding yourself as a way of life? That's not God's intention for you. There comes a time when you fight back.

I have a friend who is a former UFC champion. He told me something he would say to himself before a fight: "Survive the assault; work the cut."

Survive the assault means that when you're taking a beating, the only goal is to survive. Don't get knocked out or choked out in that round.

The second half, *work the cut*, is about offense. It means focusing on the area where the opponent is weak or injured. You don't try to knock them out with every punch, but instead you just keep breaking them down, one blow at a time.

After you survive the assault, there will be time to go on offense. That's when you work the cut.

When the angel of the Lord came to Gideon, the first thing he said was, "The Lord is with you, mighty warrior" (Judges 6:12). He was saying, "Gideon, you're a great warrior, and you've survived the assault. Now it's time to work the cut."

But Gideon was stuck in survival mode, so he ignored the compliment and brought up a complaint: "If the Lord is with us, why has all this happened to us?" (verse 13). In other words, there was no way God was with them because they were going through too much pain.

Do you ever let your complaints cancel out God's compliments? I do. I can have my mind so focused on what is missing or broken in me that when God tries to tell me what I am capable of, I downplay the opportunity and exaggerate the obstacles.

God told Gideon, "Go in the strength you have and save Israel out of Midian's hand. Am I not sending you?" (verse 14).

But Gideon pushed back again. "How can I save Israel? My clan is the weakest in Manasseh, and I am the least in my family" (verse 15).

Okay, can you hear echoes of a lizard in there? Can you see how Gideon was talking himself out of his own calling? He was so focused on how weak, young, and powerless he was that he was talking back to *God*.

And...I can't criticize him. I've been stuck in lizard land before. I've had seasons of assault that lasted so long I almost forgot to work the cut when the time came.

Maybe you've been there too. You might be there right now. It's hard to see the strength within you if you are trapped in a winepress of depression, anxiety, or loneliness.

God wants to speak to you in the winepress, though—just like he did for Gideon. I believe he wants to meet with you wherever you are. To give you a new sense of hope and mission. To show you the opportunity that's in front of you.

What will you do with what he's asking of you? Will you listen to his voice—or to the voice of insecurity, of complaint, of worst-case scenarios? Will you believe the lizard or the Lord?

I wish I could say that I always get this right, but I don't. And that's exactly why this mindset is my favorite. I have to remind myself all the time that God is not against me, but he's in it with me, working through me, fighting for me.

Sometimes we get the enemy wrong. We think *we're* the enemy: the flaws, the mistakes, the things that are messed up about us. We're embarrassed by them. We think they have to change before God can use us.

Let me tell you something I believe with all my heart. There is nothing wrong with you that can't be worked through. God's calling isn't based on your abilities or resources, but on his knowledge and power.

> There is nothing wrong with you that can't be worked through.

Remember, Gideon was *hiding* when God said, "You are a mighty warrior!" He was *whining in a winepress* when God said, "Go in the strength you have." Gideon was not the obvious choice to be the main character in this story. Not by a long shot. But God chose him even though he wouldn't have chosen himself.

He does the same with you and me.

Why? Because he never confuses who you are with where you're at. You can be in a horrible fight with a friend, but God knows you're a loving person. You can be in a rotten mood, but God sees the joy and peace within you. He sees *the true you*, not just how you're acting this minute or what you're going through today.

> God sees *the true you*, not just how you're acting this minute or what you're going through today.

Somebody told me recently that if I could see me like they see me, I wouldn't be so hard on myself. I asked what they meant, and they said, "I see you through eyes of love."

I wondered, *If they see me through eyes of love, and if God sees me through eyes of love—shouldn't I see myself through eyes of love?*

I don't, though. I usually see myself through eyes of self-criticism and self-doubt. Why? Because I know myself all too well.

Or do I?

Do I know the me I've seen up until now, or do I know the true me? Do I know the miserable me or the mighty me? The whining me or the warrior me? The hidden, hesitant me or the go-in-the-strength-God-gave-me me?

When you follow God, he doesn't just reveal himself to you. He reveals *you* to you. Not the old you, which is the you you've always known, but the true you—the version of you that he sees.

Then he speaks to your true self: "You're a mighty warrior. I see you that way. I made you that way. I put a lot of things in you that you haven't seen yet because you've been hiding from them, but you're about to discover them. Now go in the strength you have."

You've got to *go*, though. To discover your strength, you have to move forward in response to what God has said.

A while back, my son Elijah was playing *Fortnite*, and I heard him yelling into his headset, "Bro, stop camping. Stop camping! Come on, man, that's lame!"

I asked him why he was yelling, and he told me a camper is someone who doesn't really play the game; they just hide out and snipe from a distance. They don't engage, don't take a risk, don't do anything but survive.

I wonder, how often does God come calling, only to find me camping? Am I content to stay huddled over my harvest, trying to keep my stuff from getting stolen? To take a few shots from a distance but never get in the game, never take a risk, never discover what I'm capable of?

Remember, it's harder for the enemy to hit a moving target. Often the answer to the fear you feel isn't to stay still but to get going.

God was telling Gideon, "Stop camping. Be a moving target. If the enemy is going to come after you, don't let him find you in the winepress. Let him find you on the field of battle—then watch what I do through you."

I want you to say this out loud: "It may end in failure, but I will not live in fear." I know it sounds a little negative on the surface. I don't mean that I am a failure or that I expect to fail. I just mean that I don't know how my story is going to go. No one does.

I'm sure I'll fail more than a few times, but I'm not going to live scared. If I do take some damage, I want to fail while I'm fighting, not get hit while I'm hiding.

I don't know if I'm going to win great victories in every season. I don't know if I'm going to climb up or fall down when I try something new. You don't know either. We'll probably do a little bit of both.

But if God is with us, we have to walk out of the winepress. We won't find out until we step out. If we're going to get attacked by the enemy, let it happen while we're moving toward something that's worth achieving.

Haters are gonna hate. Critics are gonna criticize. Lizards are gonna lie. That's what they do. But you don't have to listen to them. They can't overrule what God says about you.

If God is for you, no demon or devil, lie or lizard, or fear or foe can win against you. He's on your side and he's got your back. He's in it with you, working through you, fighting for you.

FIFTEEN

DON'T SAY THAT

My children have a problem with closing doors. Cupboard doors, pantry doors, the front door, the back door, the garage door—they stay open until I stomp by and shut them.

I still hear my mom's voice in my head when I see one of the doors to the house left open. "Shut the door!" she'd yell when we were kids and the air conditioner was running on a hot summer day. "The cold air is getting out and the flies are getting in."

I was walking through our house the other day, just closing doors. Meanwhile, I was giving a sarcastic speech under my breath. "Yeah, sure, this is fine. I'll be the official door closer around here. I've got nothing better to do. I love to follow y'all around and close all the doors so the dumb dog y'all made me buy doesn't get out and get hit by a car."

Suddenly a thought went through my mind. *What would happen if I paid this much attention to what I let into my heart and out of my mouth? I'm so worried about letting flies in, but I let fear in. I'm so bothered about letting the cold air out, but I let negativity and anger out.*

I didn't stop being irritated, and I kept slamming doors a little harder than I needed to, but it made me think. I remembered the verse that says, "Above all else, guard your heart, for everything you do flows from it" (Proverbs 4:23).

If we aren't careful, we can let all kinds of things get into our hearts. Bad news can make us spiral into doom and despair. A minor setback in our plans can throw us into emotional chaos. A slight offense can turn into a feeling of total rejection.

With just a thought or two, we let faith leak out and we let fear rush in. We lose our confidence because we lose control of our internal conversation.

> We lose our confidence because we lose control of our internal conversation.

Now, I'm not saying to lie about what is happening around you. Don't pretend everything is fine if it's not. What I'm saying is, don't leave the door wide open to negativity and doubt. When bad news comes, tell yourself, "Yes, this sucks. But God is in it with me. He's still working through me, and he's going to fight for me."

When God called Jeremiah to be a prophet, Jeremiah didn't believe he was capable of stepping into God's destiny. He was too discouraged by his low view of himself to trust God's vision for him. So he said, "Alas, Sovereign Lord, I do not know how to speak; I am too young" (Jeremiah 1:6).

I've heard responses like this from my kids more times than I can remember. "I can't. It's too hard. I don't know how."

The truth is, I've watched them figure out things from technology to musical theory so much faster than me, I know it's less about ability and more about believing in themselves.

I've been a parent long enough to know that some of their "reasons" are excuses to get out of something they don't want to do. So I'll say to them, "Yes, you can do it. Here, I'll show you how for the twentieth time. Then you're going to do what I know you're capable of doing." Or sometimes I just take out the trash myself because it's easier. And because I know they'll leave the pantry door open.

When it comes to Jeremiah, I don't blame him for making excuses. I'm sure he was scared of the calling that God had for him. But his arguments were a smoke screen that stopped him from seeing his true self.

God said to Jeremiah, "Do not say, 'I am too young.' You must go to everyone I send you to and say whatever I command you. Do not be afraid of them, for I am with you and will rescue you" (verses 7–8).

Jeremiah believed his own excuses, but God saw past them. Just like he does when we try to deny who we really are.

Brendon Burchard, a friend of mine and personal development coach, says there are three main excuses we make for not stepping into our potential:

> "I don't have it."
> "I don't know how."
> "I'm not like them."

Jeremiah's arguments fit into all three of those categories. "I don't have the skill or respect. I don't know how to speak well. I'm not like other prophets; I'm too young and inexperienced." He assumed he was going to fail so that he didn't have to risk actually failing.

Do you ever do that? I do. About five times a day. On a good day. No sooner does an idea pop into my head than four other thoughts appear to tell me why it won't work and how unqualified I am to do it anyway.

I find myself using these three phrases far more often than I should, and I wonder if you might too. They don't sound like excuses when we say them—they sound like logic. But God knows they are excuses. And he says, "Yes, you can do it. Here, I'll show you how for the twentieth time. Then you're going to do what I know you're capable of doing."

First, you might say, *"I don't have it."* When you say this, you're often talking about a lack of resources. You don't have the skill to play on the team. You don't have the grades to get a scholarship. You don't have a car to drive to a part-time job.

The true you doesn't quit just because you don't have enough, though. Instead, you say, "I don't have enough now, but I'll have it when I need it. So I'm going to take the first step. The God who supplies all my needs according to his riches in glory is with me."

The second excuse is, *"I don't know how."* This one uses your lack of knowledge, skill, or experience to keep you from trying to do things that are outside your comfort zone. You never learned how to play an instrument. You never tried out for drama club. You don't know how to fill out college applications.

The other day I asked a friend of mine if he would ever consider learning to play the guitar because he loves the guitar so much. He said, "No, at this stage in my life, I'm too old to suck at something." He didn't even try because he didn't want to deal with the mistakes that come with learning something new.

But why should ignorance or inexperience get the final word? You've been learning since the day you were born, and you'll keep learning until the day you die. In the age of Google, YouTube, and ChatGPT, "I don't know how" is more likely to be a cover-up for fear or laziness than an actual obstacle.

The true you looks at failure and starting points differently. You're willing to learn along the way, even if that means being embarrassed or changing your mind about some things as you grow.

Finally, the third excuse is, *"I'm not like them."* This is about comparison. It's a feeling of not being enough—the infamous imposter syndrome—that makes you disqualify yourself because you think others are something you are not.

Again, though, that's the old you. The true you knows that the unique way God made you is part of the reason he chose you. The true you says, "My difference *is* my strength. I don't have to hide or change. God made me who I am for a reason. He put me here for such a time as this."

> The true you knows that the unique way God made you is part of the reason he chose you.

Besides, when you say, "I'm not like them," what you really mean is, "I'm not like the version of them that I imagine based on what I see." Most people are just curating the parts of themselves they want you to notice. Don't allow your impression of someone else to become your insecurity about yourself.

Listen to God's reply to Jeremiah. "Do not say, 'I am too young.' You must go to everyone I send you to and say whatever I command you. Do not be afraid of them, for I am with you and will rescue you" (verses 7–8).

God was saying, "Jeremiah, people might be against you, but I am with you and for you. I've put my words and strength within you. I will fight for you, and nobody will defeat you, because I will save you."

God was in it with him, working through him, and fighting for him. That was God's answer to Jeremiah's arguments.

And it's his answer to our arguments too.

When you say, "I'm not," or "I'm only," or "I can't" to a God who is calling you into your future, you're letting out something that's way more valuable than air-conditioning. You lose out on the potential God has given you when you speak words that limit you.

> You lose out on the potential God has given you when you speak words that limit you.

When we were first starting our church, I remember a conversation that changed the way I saw myself. I was talking with Tyler, our volunteer creative director, about the next sermon series I was going to preach. I had an idea for artwork to go with the series. So I said, "Tyler, I know I'm not really creative, but I was wondering if..." Then I described my idea.

When I finished, he said, "That's a great idea, and I think we should do it. But there's one thing I wish you would never do again."

I thought maybe he was going to say, "Don't tell me how

to design sermon artwork. You do the preaching. I'll do the design."

But he didn't. What he said was much more challenging than that. He said, "Please don't say you're not creative. You're one of the most creative people I've ever met. Just because you don't know how to use Photoshop doesn't mean you're not creative. And I wish you'd stop saying it."

I was twenty-five at the time. It's weird for me to think back to that version of myself. Although I still struggle with my inner critic (as you've seen), I *do* accept myself as creative now. I'm made in the image of God. How could I not be creative? I'm so glad Tyler had the guts to speak up and say, "Don't say that."

Are you undermining your potential with the words you let out of your mouth? Are you allowing thoughts that sabotage your confidence and stifle your creativity to wander unchecked through your mind?

If so, be like Tyler. Call yourself out on what you're saying about yourself. Don't make flippant comments that lock you into the old you. "I'm not good at that. I could never do that. I'm not…I can't…I won't…"

If God has called you, he will be with you. And if he is with you, you'll have what you need, when you need it.

Instead of *I don't have it*, declare, "God knows what I need before I even ask, and his provision is already on the way."

Instead of *I don't know how*, say, "The steps of a good person are guided by the Lord, so he'll lead me as I walk this out."

Instead of *I'm not like them*, tell yourself, "I am who I am by the grace of God, and I'm enough for whatever is ahead of me."

Close the doors that are letting in the fear and letting out the confidence. Don't speak things that kill your dreams or silence your voice. Don't say things that pull you back into the old way of doing you.

> Close the doors that are letting in the fear and letting out the confidence.

Speak life over yourself. Speak grace and hope. Speak what God sees in you and what he says about you.

"I am called, and I am chosen. I might be young, I might be inexperienced, I might be overlooked, I might make some mistakes—but I will walk in confidence because God is not against me, but he's in it with me, working through me, fighting for me."

SIXTEEN

GOD IS UP TO SOMETHING UPSTREAM

Over the years I've had the chance to write songs with some amazing people. That includes my friend Brandon Lake, who lives a few hours away from me.

We were writing songs one day and he said, "I've never told you this before, but about twelve years ago, when I was eighteen years old, I emailed Elevation Church and asked if I could come learn about songwriting. I was told, 'No, sorry,' by somebody who doesn't work here anymore. So I gave up on it, but I never forgot about it. And now here we are, writing songs together."

I didn't know that part of Brandon's story, and it got me thinking. I remembered one time, years ago, sitting in my office and feeling overwhelmed by everything I had to do. We were a young church, but we were large enough that I was managing way too much. That included planning the Sunday worship set and other technical details.

Even then, I felt like God had put a promise in my heart that our worship songs and albums were going to go around the world. But there I was, hunched over my laptop, putting together chord charts and trying not to get stressed out about everything else I had to do. It didn't seem like we were anywhere close to touching the world.

I had no idea that a few miles away, in Charleston, South Carolina, God was raising up a young man named Brandon, who was going to write his own songs that would go all over the world, and who I would get to collaborate with in amazing ways. I had no idea how many other incredible singers, musicians, and writers I would get to work with, year after year, right here within our own church. But God did.

While I was worrying, God was working. While I was praying about something, God was preparing something.

I just couldn't see it yet.

I wonder how often the answer to our prayers and our problems is a few miles or a few months away—but we can't see what God is doing, so we feel alone. We feel left behind.

In those moments, we have to choose faith over feelings. That's what the true you would do. You would walk in confidence, knowing that God is in it with you, and he's up to something you can't see.

> Choose faith over feelings. That's what the true you would do.

Remember how God told Israel to cross the Jordan River and enter the Promised Land? There was a problem, though. It was flood season, so the river was deeper, wider, and faster than normal. The idea of moving an entire nation across it, including children, livestock, and possessions, would have been completely overwhelming.

God already had a plan, though. He told Joshua to command the priests to carry the ark of the covenant into the river. Joshua promised everyone that the water would stop flowing so they could cross. But when the priests and the ark started moving, the water was still rushing as fast as ever.

Now, just imagine the conversations the people were having right then. They were walking toward the floodwaters in faith, but they still hadn't seen the miracle. They could only follow the ark, which represented God's presence among them. The ark was God "in it with them." It was the promise that God would work through them and fight for them.

Here's how the Bible describes what happened when the priests reached the river. "Now the Jordan is at flood stage all during harvest. Yet as soon as the priests who carried the ark reached the Jordan and their feet touched the water's edge, the water from upstream stopped flowing. It piled up in a heap a great distance away, at a town called Adam in the vicinity of Zarethan, while the water flowing down to the Sea of the Arabah (that is, the Dead Sea) was completely cut off. So the people crossed over opposite Jericho" (Joshua 3:15–16).

When the priests' feet touched the Jordan, the water stopped flowing. Not when they prayed about the Jordan. Not when they read three books about the Jordan. When they *stepped into the Jordan*. By walking toward uncertainty, they demonstrated their faith for victory.

But they didn't see it till they got there.

They had to step out in faith.

That's where you are going to see the miracle: as you walk forward into God's calling, even if it's awkward and uncomfortable. You keep praying, keep believing, keep trusting, keep showing up even when it feels scary or hopeless

> That's where you are going to see the miracle: as you walk forward into God's calling, even if it's awkward and uncomfortable.

because you know God is with you. You keep reading your Bible instead of mindlessly scrolling. You keep inviting that kid when no one else does. You keep practicing the skill you haven't mastered yet. You keep refusing to drink at that party. You keep protecting your purity.

I realized a while back that I'd been reading the story wrong. I always pictured it like the Red Sea: Israel is backed up against the water, the people step into the river, the water stands up into two giant walls, and they walk through.

But that's not what the Bible says happened here. It says, "The water from upstream stopped flowing. It piled up in a heap a great distance away" (verse 16).

That means the water had already stopped flowing upstream so they could cross downstream. It was an *upstream* miracle. One that had happened hours earlier—at just the right time. They were wondering how they would cross the river downstream while God was already up to something upstream.

This is what I want you to see: You have an upstream God! Your trust is in a God who knew what you'd be facing long before you got there. He's prepared you for this moment and this moment for you.

I don't know about you, but I prefer a foolproof, detailed plan before I take a single step. Sometimes Holly will tell me, "Let's go on a walk. It's beautiful outside." The first thing I do is check the weather app. What if it rains while we're walking around the block? Holly will say, "Babe, it's a walk around the block. We're not hiking the Appalachian Trail. And if it does rain, we have towels at home when we get back."

I'm a work in progress. I'm learning to let go of the need to know every obstacle I might face because that's really just a need for control. And my need for control can keep me from going forward. Sometimes it costs me a walk around the block, but sometimes it costs me an opportunity that's much bigger.

I have to remind myself that God is in control. I don't need complete knowledge of the weather forecast, and I don't need complete knowledge of the road of life that lies ahead. I just need faith to trust him and strength to follow him.

What are you stepping toward right now? Maybe you're going to be the first person in your family to go to college, so you're stepping into it even though you don't have an example of it. As you step, you're getting stronger and the path is getting clearer.

The story of Israel wading into the water is a picture of step-taking faith, which is real faith. Sometimes I think we look at faith like it's a feeling. When we say, "I have faith this will work out," it can mean, "I have a good feeling about this."

That's not what I need when I'm facing an overflowing Jordan, though. What I *don't* have when I'm on the bank of a river at flood stage is "a good feeling about this."

I need faith that will help me step through something I *don't* have a good feeling about. I need faith to help me step into difficult situations when I don't see how God could possibly work all things together for good.

The good news of the gospel is that this faith doesn't

come from us—it was given to us by God. The Bible says, "For it is by grace you have been saved, through faith—and this is not from yourselves, it is the gift of God" (Ephesians 2:8). Grace is what saves us; faith is what allows us to receive that grace; and *both* come from above.

That means faith isn't something you have to work up or make up. Yes, you'll need to abide in faith, walk in faith, and grow in faith. But since it's a gift from God, it's more about him than about you. It'll just keep coming with every step and in every situation because God is always up to something upstream.

The town of Adam, where the water started piling up, was about twenty miles up the river. How long does it take water to flow twenty miles? Six hours, maybe? I don't know—but God did.

Think about the timing of God. The moment their feet got wet, the water dried up. That means God got to Adam six hours before Israel got to the Jordan.

He said, "Hey, Jordan River, stop right now because in six hours, the priests' feet are going to hit the water. In six hours, they're going to be on the brink of the promise I made to Abraham four hundred years ago."

Israel had no way of knowing what was happening upstream. Nobody in Adam was texting them saying, "Hey, the water has been piling up in a heap here, so y'all get ready to cross because the Jordan is going to dry up downstream any minute now."

They couldn't plan it or time it. They could only step into it when God told them to start moving.

So ask yourself, "What is something I know God has spoken to me that I can obey today?"

Then do that thing.

When you don't know how to stand or what to do, start doing the thing that you would do if you knew God was in it with you, working through you, fighting for you. Do the thing you would do if you believed he's been working upstream all along.

"But I'm not certain how it's going to turn out." Well, do the thing that you would do if you were certain that God was with you.

"Are you saying I could just start anything and assume that God is with me? Can I become a music artist and sell millions of albums because the Lord is going to bless whatever I do?" I don't know. You might not know how to write music, and I've never heard you play or sing, so that's between you, God, and people who can give you some honest feedback. But if he's calling you to step into a promise he gave you, then do the thing that you would do if you knew he was already at work twenty miles upstream.

You don't know what God is up to upstream. That's why you can't die downstream. That's why you have to step into the Jordan. That's why you have to do the thing that you would do if you believed victory, healing, second chances, and new beginnings were on the other side. Remember, wherever you have a problem, heaven has a plan. Turn the outcome over to the Lord and leave it there.

> Wherever you have a problem, heaven has a plan.

Then, take the step.

Will you trust him with the twenty miles in between? Will you try not to stress for the next three days while you wait for your test result? While your application to your dream college is being processed, can you believe that God's already at work on your behalf? While they continue to say mean things about you, can you choose to remain silent and kind, knowing God is fighting for you?

You're going to have some downstream doubts. When you can't see what God's doing, you'll wonder sometimes if you're crazy for trusting him.

Doubts don't indicate lack of faith, though. They're just feelings, and feelings come and go. Faith is deeper than that and more visible than that. Faith is about action. So do what *the true you* would do: the you who God is speaking to. The you who is in sync with him. The you who is full of faith.

Maybe you're standing on the bank of the river, about to dip your big toe into it. Maybe you're going to call a therapist this week and say, "I'm ready to start working on my issues." Maybe you're going to reach out to a friend with an apology. Maybe you're going to buy a canvas and paints because something inside you is telling you to keep doing your art. Maybe you'll text back that person who reached out to you because you're tired of being lonely and she might make a good friend.

Those are steps. That is faith.

While you're taking baby steps into rushing rivers, God is up to mighty miracles twenty miles away. He's preparing things you can't see and don't expect. It might not happen in the next two days or two months. That's okay—the timeframe is God's business. But if you can believe him, if you can take the steps the true you would take, you're going to see the miracle.

You can't control the river, but you can walk toward it. You can step into it. And when you do, you'll find out what God has been up to all along.

SEVENTEEN

MAKE PEACE WITH YOUR STRENGTH

Growing up in the South, I collected a long list of interesting sayings. For example, "You're getting too big for your britches" means you're starting to think a little too highly of yourself. For some reason I heard that a lot as a teenager.

Later in life, when I was studying to be a pastor, a religious version of the phrase was instilled in me. It usually went along with Proverbs 16:18. "Pride goes before destruction, a haughty spirit before a fall."

Basically what was communicated was that if you did something good, you needed to give God all the credit; and if you did something bad, you better take all the blame. I'm not saying this was taught directly, but you just kind of picked it up. You could talk about your failures all you wanted because that was humility. But you had to be careful when you talked about what you had accomplished because you might be getting caught up in pride—and that sin got the devil kicked out of heaven.

To this day, when I celebrate good things that happen, I

often find myself subconsciously worried that I'm getting too big for my britches. I wonder if God is going to humble me somehow just to put me in my place.

Now, it's definitely a bad idea to think you did something all on your own when God enabled you to do it, or to allow an accomplishment to make you think you're better than someone else, or to assume you're above tripping and falling around the next corner.

But the idea that I shouldn't feel good about something I've done is kind of messed up, isn't it? What if my kids viewed me the same way I've often viewed God? "Be careful what you say around Dad. If he thinks you're proud of what you've accomplished, if he sees you taking credit for your good grades or your wrestling trophy or a picture you drew, he'll take you down a notch. He'll humble you just to teach you a lesson."

Can you see how toxic that belief is? That's why the first part of this affirmation—"God is not against me"—is foundational to the rest of it. If we are going to walk in faith, if we are going to be and do all the things God has put inside us, we can't start from a place of "God is out to get me." That's a path that leads to paralysis, not possibility.

I know I owe everything to God's grace. I've worked hard and done my best, but I could never do enough to deserve all the blessings and opportunities God has given me. I don't for a moment think I can work my way into heaven. I know that pride is a sneaky, subtle enemy and staying humble is my responsibility.

But along with all that, God has been teaching me to think differently about the talents and abilities he's given me.

He's teaching me to make peace not just with my weaknesses or mistakes, but with my strengths. With my gifts. With my calling.

I believe he's asking the same thing of you. I think he gets excited when you do great things, and it makes him proud. Why? Because he's your father, and fathers—good fathers—are naturally proud of their kids.

For example, I'm proud that my son Elijah released three albums by the time he was nineteen. They aren't platinum-selling albums, of course. He's just getting started, and he's going to get better and better as he makes music throughout his life. But the fact that he put two albums into the world with songs he wrote and recorded himself is worth celebrating.

As I watched him work on album art, push through insecurity to shoot music videos, and find his own confidence as he combined the music he loves with his life experience, I never felt the need to "bring him down a notch." I didn't try to make sure he gave me enough credit for buying his recording equipment or for encouraging him through the process. He's my son, and he's stepping into his calling and gifting and dreams, and that makes me happy. He's a work in progress, but as his father, I celebrated every step.

How much more excited do you think God gets when you use the strengths he gave you? He loves to see you step into the potential he put inside you. Can you imagine that? Can you imagine God being proud of you? Complimenting you? Promoting you? Celebrating you?

Because that's what he does. That's who he is. That's how he thinks. That's how he sees you.

When Proverbs says that pride goes before destruction, it doesn't mean God wants you to call yourself a worm and grovel in the dirt. It just means you shouldn't get arrogant and think everything you have is because you're so awesome, smart, and strong. It means that while you walk in your *strength*, you keep trusting in your *God*. Those two things should work together.

That's what I mean by making peace with your strength. It's not pride to see your strengths. It's a perspective of faith.

Are you an artist? Are you good at math? Are you a people person? Do you come up with creative ideas? Do you like public speaking? Are you athletic? Do you love solving problems? Do you bring joy to a room? Do you have the ability to make other people feel included?

Those are not minor details. Those are not accidental qualities. God put strength in you. He knows it—and hopefully you know it too. You need to be willing to walk in those gifts without thinking God is going to send a lightning bolt to zap you if you dare to dream big.

A lot of people talk about the importance of accepting your weaknesses and being okay with who you are. There's a place for all of that, and we've discussed it quite a bit in this book. But self-acceptance should include your strengths too.

Don't just say, "Look at all the things I can't do. I'm just going to sit around and watch other people do stuff on YouTube for hours rather than trying to do anything myself." No, you have to notice your gifts. You have to value your dreams. You have to pay attention to your skills and the doors God has set before you.

I think sometimes we don't make peace with our

strengths because we know that if we do, we're responsible to use them. But if we use them, we might fail. So to avoid that, it feels easier to say that the time isn't right, that we need more experience, that someone else would do the job better.

As we saw earlier, that's exactly what Gideon tried to do when God first called him. I want to look at his story again because Gideon was really good at accepting his weaknesses, but he had a harder time accepting his strengths.

Remember, at the beginning of the story, the angel and Gideon had a little argument. The angel said Gideon was a mighty warrior, and Gideon ignored that and said God had abandoned them. So the angel ignored *that* and said, "Go in the strength you have and save Israel out of Midian's hand. Am I not sending you?" Finally Gideon replied, "But how can I save Israel? My clan is the weakest in Manasseh, and I am the least in my family" (Judges 6:14–15).

Do you see how hard Gideon was fighting *not* to believe in himself? How passionately he defended a low view of his potential because that seemed safer than recognizing the gifts and callings God had given him?

God doesn't lose arguments, though. He finally convinced Gideon to see the true version of himself and to believe God was with him, and he became one of the greatest leaders in Israel's history.

What about you? Are you arguing with a God who sees the strengths he gave you and won't stop until you see them too? If so, will you let him win? Or will you shrink down to the level of your past, to your doubts, to the insecurity that keeps you stuck inside yourself?

Like Gideon, you can be strong and weak at the same

time. One doesn't cancel out the other: They're meant to coexist. That's why you have to accept them both.

The weakness teaches you to depend on Jesus. If you didn't have any weakness, you would think you didn't need Jesus, and you probably *would* get too big for your britches.

The strength exists to show you what God and you can do together. It gives you confidence to say, "I can do all things through Christ, who strengthens me." It gives you faith in a God who does far more than you can ask or imagine through his power that works in you.

For Gideon, the turning point in the argument came when he offered the angel something to eat. The angel touched the food with his staff, and fire instantly burned up the meal. Gideon realized this wasn't just your average angel he was talking to—it was God himself. Immediately he was filled with fear because he had seen God face-to-face.

Can I tell you something? When God shows us who he really is and tells us what we can do through his presence and power, the first thing we often feel is fear. I know fear gets a bad rap, but it doesn't always mean that something is wrong. Sometimes it's just a natural reaction to God breaking through our senses and our limited experience and showing up in our situation.

So if you find fear rising up when you face something challenging, don't duck back into the winepress. Don't hide in who you used to be. God is calling you into the true you, and that will take a little getting used to.

God told Gideon, "Peace! Do not be afraid. You are not going to die" (verse 23). Then Gideon built an altar on the spot and called it "The Lord Is Peace" (verse 24).

Think about that for a moment. God showed up, the food burned up, Gideon got all worked up—and then he realized this was *friendly* fire. God wasn't there to judge him but to anoint him. Like Moses at the burning bush, like the flames of fire at Pentecost, this was God showing up in his all-consuming love and power to call Gideon into his true self.

Making peace with your strength starts by knowing God is at peace with you. He's not against you; he's for you. The peace you have *with* God and *in* God is what gives you confidence to carry out his purpose.

> Making peace with your strength starts by knowing God is at peace with you.

You can say, "God, these are the gifts you've given me. Sometimes I don't feel like much, but you're calling me mighty, and you're saying I have strengths, so I'm going to go in whatever I've got."

Maybe you find yourself thinking, *I could be a more patient person. I could be more encouraging. I could try out for that team. I could apply for that summer job.* Maybe you could! Go in the strength you have and find out. Don't disqualify yourself by quitting before you even have a chance to succeed. Don't hide in a winepress and call it humility if God is telling you to move forward in faith.

> Don't disqualify yourself by quitting before you even have a chance to succeed.

Making peace with your strength isn't easy. Sometimes you can minimize what God is doing so it fits it into your past experience. God is calling you up higher, but if he is saying something about you that you've never seen in you, it might scare you. "I can't do that. That's not me."

But what if it *is* you? What if the other stuff—the fear, the holding back, the negativity, the worry, the not being creative, the not wanting to lead, the lack of follow-through—is the false stuff? What if "wimp in a winepress" is just where fear has put you, but "mighty warrior" is who God calls you?

If you read the rest of the story, God did an incredible miracle through Gideon and three hundred soldiers. They didn't have a massive army, and they didn't even have real weapons, but they had faith. Faith in a God who was for them, not against them. Faith in a God who worked through them and fought on their side.

Sometimes when God calls you a mighty warrior, you start looking around for a mighty army. Maybe there isn't one. The might isn't in the size of the army—it's in the size of the God in you. It's Christ in you. That has always been enough, and it will always make you enough.

Make peace with your strength because the God of Peace gave it to you. Don't fight the fire God has given you. Don't fake things just to impress people who won't be in your life in five years. Don't downplay yourself to fit in with friends who aren't going where God is taking you.

Yes, you'll feel fear at times. But the answer isn't to hide out and hope someone else answers the call. It's to take a step forward even while you still feel afraid. It's to grow into everything God says you are. Accept your Self, the one he created you to be, and rely on him.

Do the thing *that* you would do. The mighty warrior you. The capable you. The called you. The confident you. The you that has made peace with your strength.

What you tell yourself matters, which is why it's so important to remind yourself that God is not against you, but he's in it with you,

> What you tell yourself matters.

working through you, fighting for you. The more you can believe that affirmation, the more confidence you'll have as you step into your future.

One of the greatest challenges you face as you take these steps of faith is to guard your heart and mind from negative self-talk. I'm not talking about ignoring reality. I'm talking about making sure you don't look at life through the wrong filters: things like doubt, fear, insecurity, negativity, and hopelessness.

And that brings us to our next mindset. It's the shortest but maybe the most practical of them all: *My joy is my job.*

MINDSET (05)

MY JOY IS MY JOB.

ACTION STEP:
OWN YOUR EMOTIONS.

EIGHTEEN

THE HARD WORK OF HAPPINESS

A few years ago, while we were on vacation, I asked my family, "Who's the happiest person you know?" I'm famous for starting games like this—and my kids are famous for pointing out the problems with them.

They said, "Dad, that's an impossible question. You can't know if people are actually happy or not."

They had a point. But I kept pushing, so they started listing the happiest people they knew. I was surprised by some of their answers, but I was not surprised that none of them said, "You, Dad."

Don't get me wrong. I can be a pretty fun guy. But I wasn't expecting to get the Happiest Human Alive Award, or even the Happiest Dad Award, for that matter. Still, part of me was hoping at least one of them would give me an honorable mention. After all, I was paying for their vacation. I had even ordered appetizers.

So before it was Holly's turn, I tried to drop a hint and

make it easy for her. I said, "Holly, *you* are the happiest person I know." It wasn't flattery: it was true.

She replied, "That's so sweet." And then she said somebody else's name as her answer.

The conversation gave me a lot to think about. I've been told more than once that I have a tendency to look...serious, shall I say. Or mad. Or even mean. Some people's natural expression is "resting blessed face." I have the other kind of RBF, apparently.

And if I'm honest, I'm *not* an automatically optimistic person. My first instinct in any situation is to see what's potentially dangerous about it or wrong with it. And if I can't find anything, I'll keep looking, because I am highly skilled at finding stuff to worry about. That's the guy who Holly, the happiest person I know, gets to live with.

A man named Brian Wilson who was a member of a band called the Beach Boys once said, "I'm seventy years old and it took me a long time to learn a really simple thing: it's hard work to be happy."* I get that. I've realized it's not easy to own my emotions. It's hard work to handle my feelings.

That's why I lean into this liberating little phrase: *My joy is my job.*

I say it to myself a lot, and it's a good reminder to keep my feelings and attitude under control. The Bible says, "This is the day the Lord has made; We will rejoice and be glad in

---

* "Rock & Roll Music Legend Brian Wilson to Publish New Memoir with Random House Canada," news release, Random House of Canada Limited, April 15, 2013. https://www.newswire.ca/news-releases/rock—roll-music-legend-brian-wilson-to-publish-new-memoir-with-random-house-canada-512265701.html.

it" (Psalm 118:24 NKJV). *Will rejoice* means joy is an act of the will. In other words, it's within our control. We get to choose the energy we carry into our day.

I like calling it the "hard work of happiness" because you have to work at it sometimes. (Some of us more than others, apparently.) We usually don't think about it that way, though. We assume happiness should be easy. That we should wake up in the morning with a bounce in our step and go through our day with positive vibes only.

But it doesn't work that way. Your emotions can shift and change without warning. You can wake up excited and full of hope, then get a text message and lose your joy by 7:45 in the morning. Or you can be in a bad mood coming home after school, but a song you love comes on as you're turning into the driveway, and the negativity you carried the whole day evaporates in two seconds.

Your feelings *matter*, but feelings can be *fickle*. Both of those things are true.

They can change in an instant, and they often don't consult your permission to do so. Feelings can flip. Fast.

And that's where the work comes in.

You have to manage your emotions. You have to notice your feelings and understand how they fit into the bigger picture of who you are.

Now, I didn't say bury your feelings. I didn't say hate them, hide them, or feel guilty for them. I didn't say "just move on" after that cruel breakup or pretend you're fine if you're not. I didn't say to keep all the stress you're under bottled up inside until you hit a wall and start having panic attacks.

I said *own your emotions*. Take responsibility for your attitudes and moods. Notice the things that are rushing through your head and heart and respond to them appropriately. Intentionally. Maturely. Talk to God about them. Journal how you're feeling. Talk it out with someone you trust. Do whatever you have to do to start the process of dealing with and attempting to understand how you're feeling.

Do what the true you would do.

The old version of you thought happiness came from the outside. It was something you chased, earned, built, or demanded.

The true you knows that happiness comes from *within* you. Peace is inside you because the God of Peace is always with you. Joy, contentment, gratitude, forgiveness, freedom, and confidence are all growing within you because of the presence and power of the Holy Spirit.

Owning your emotions means that *you* are central to the process. Your joy is your job. Your attitude is your assignment. Your stability is your responsibility. Nobody else is in charge of making you happy and content.

> Nobody else is in charge of making you happy and content.

Your parents don't have that job. Or your friends. Or your teachers. Or your dog. They can be there for you, but they can't carry the weight of your happiness. Only you can answer for your attitude.

One time I made the mistake of saying somebody stole my joy, and the Holy Spirit really called me out on it. "They stole your joy? Your joy is up to you, not them. If someone else can steal your joy, that means you're keeping your joy where anybody can come along and snatch it."

ABBEY

This is a concept I struggled with for a long time. It gets really dangerous when you romanticize and find comfort in the idea of being sad. It can be easier to stay sad and for that to become who you are. It's a shortcut, an easy way out.

When you start to do that, when you blame people for "stealing your joy," it becomes your identity. If your happiness comes from people, and people hurt you, you fall into this spiral. Even if you feel that way at first, you have to find a way to get out of that headspace. It's your choice.

This mindset helps me so much when I've been hurt or betrayed by someone who genuinely made me happy. It can be easy to say, "Well, I was happiest with them, but they stole my joy, and now I can't be happy." But instead of that, if you switch the way you think and say, "How can I grow from this?" then you keep your joy safe.

This is never easy at first, but as I've practiced it, I've gotten used to managing my joy myself. I may not be the happiest person on earth, but I am confident that I no longer have sadness attached to my identity.

I might not be the happiest guy my family knows, but that doesn't mean I have to be the grumpiest one. My joy is my job, and I'm determined to be up for the task. Social media can't steal my joy. Stressful conversations can't steal my tranquility. Toxic people can't steal my contentment. All these things are mine to manage.

As I said, I had to learn how this works. I remember a few years ago, things were going really well for me. I was hitting goals and experiencing more success than ever before. But on the inside, I felt dead. The goals I was reaching felt empty, and instead of celebrating, I found myself crying. I remember going on vacation and feeling sad the entire time, like I was a prisoner in my own mind.

My lack of joy in the presence of so much goodness really scared me. On the way home from vacation, I told Holly, "I think I need to get some help. I don't think I'm in a good place."

She had told me several times that I should consider meeting with a counselor to process all the pressure I was under, but I resisted for the same reasons we often resist getting help. I thought if I just pushed through, tried harder, hit more goals, and improved my environment, my feelings and thoughts would take care of themselves. I was on that treadmill of chasing and never quite catching up with the "Future You" I talked about earlier.

The problem was inside me, though, not around me. I was burying some stuff I needed to deal with and carrying some things I needed to set down, and it was burning me out.

The old mindset was killing me and the true me was calling me—but it wouldn't come easy. First, I had to find someone to talk to, which meant admitting to another human being that I needed help. For someone who likes to be thought of as the strong one, that was hard to do.

But I did it. And that began a process of weekly therapy

that I've been committed to for years now. Today, I'm in a much better place. Not just because of therapy, but because of a commitment to the deep work of putting off old ways of doing me and putting on new ones. I've had to do the work of dealing with what was truly going on inside of me instead of deflecting and denying it.

My point isn't that you need therapy. Maybe you do, maybe you don't. My point is that regardless of the tools you use, you have to own your emotions. You have to understand some things about yourself, about your ways of processing, about your personality, about your pain.

Feelings and emotions and desires have a place, but that place is not the throne of our lives. *God* is on the throne. That means what God says about you should carry the greatest weight, even when you aren't really "feeling it."

> Feelings and emotions and desires have a place, but that place is not the throne of our lives. *God* is on the throne.

We tend to put our feelings on the throne. If we want to go off about something, we go off. If we want to sleep in, we sleep in. If we want to skip leg day, we skip leg day. If we feel like doing something sinful to feel relief in a stressful moment, we justify it: "Oh, it's not that bad." We let our feelings tell us what is true and right.

But feelings aren't meant to be followed blindly. They're meant to be taught and trained by what God says about us.

The passage we've been looking at in Ephesians 4 says that the old self "is being corrupted by its deceitful desires" (verse 22). The problem with *deceitful* desires is that, by definition, they trick you. You can have cravings, feelings, emotions, and needs that present themselves to you as absolute truth, but they aren't what they claim to be. They are sneaky. They are subtle. They are convincing. But they are not always right.

Many times in my life, I've had to face the consequences of doing things that "felt" right when I did them. I bet you have too. The anger that seemed so right in the moment. The lie that was so helpful in getting what you wanted. The gossip about someone else that made you feel better about yourself, but only for a few seconds. The slammed door that got your point across to your parents.

But at what cost?

The new, true version of you is called to see deceitful desires for what they are: flashbacks to the old you. So how do you identify which desires and feelings are deceitful? How do you walk in the new you instead of reverting to the old you?

Let me give you three simple steps. Think of the word NEW as an acronym.

> Notice
> Evaluate
> Walk In

Notice means paying attention to your thoughts, reactions, feelings, fears, and desires. In case you never go to therapy, I want to make sure you get this basic psychology foundation: You can't deal with things you don't know are there. You can't make good choices when you don't even realize you're choosing in the first place.

So pay attention to your fear. Listen to your anger. Take

note when something within you gets triggered. "There I am, blaming people again. There I am, catastrophizing again." Notice it—but then remind yourself that you're not it.

Next, *evaluate* the thing you've noticed. Is this desire good or bad? Is this action right or wrong? Is this decision wise or unwise? Don't just shrug your shoulders and say, "That's just me. That's how I've always been. That's how my dad is too. Oh well." Compare that thing to what God says about you. Evaluate whether it's the new you or the old you.

When fear comes, I try to frame it this way in my mind: "I'm feeling fear." This gives me some separation from my emotion so I can deal with the fear for what it is. If I say, "I *am* afraid," that pushes me toward an identity. I don't want to be Scared Steven. Scared Steven does dumb things. He lashes out, he snaps at people, he makes shortsighted decisions. On the other hand, if I say, "I'm *feeling* fear," then I'm simply acknowledging a fact. The emotion is real, but it's not going to last forever. It's like stormy weather—it will pass. It's not who I am. Jesus is in me, and Jesus isn't scared, so Scared Steven isn't the real me.

I *notice* the fear like I would check the weather. I *evaluate* it. Then I *walk in* the me that I'm meant to be, carrying an umbrella if I have to. I choose to walk in faith and courage because that's the true me.

In Christ, your joy is not held hostage by anything or anyone. It's yours. Your joy comes from Jesus—not from the world. And as the old gospel song says, "If the world didn't give it, the world can't take it away."*

---

* Written and performed by Shirley Caesar, "The World Didn't Give It to Me" (HOB, 1975).

Jesus told his disciples, "Peace I leave with you; my peace I give you. I do not give to you as the world gives. Do not let your hearts be troubled and do not be afraid" (John 14:27). Later he said to them, "You will grieve, but your grief will turn to joy...I will see you again and you will rejoice, and no one will take away your joy" (John 16:20, 22).

Even when the world is shifting and quaking around you, God gives you a peace that the world can't give you. He gives you a joy nobody can steal from you.

> God gives you a peace that the world can't give you. He gives you a joy nobody can steal from you.

You don't have to be the most cheerful, extroverted, life-of-the-party person on the outside. That's okay. Your family loves you anyway.

On the inside, though, you can know that your joy is real, and it's yours, and you're growing more and more each day into the image of Christ in you.

NINETEEN

WHO'S IN YOUR HEAD?

Joey Logano is a NASCAR driver and two-time Cup Series champion. He's a friend of our family and part of our church, and I'm a big fan of his, even though I don't know a lot about NASCAR.

The first time I took my family to a race, it was because Joey talked me into it. I was a little unsure about it at first. I said, "I totally respect what you do, but wouldn't it be kind of boring to watch you drive around in circles for four hours?"

He said, "Trust me, bring the kids. They'll love it."

We met his crew at the Charlotte Motor Speedway, and they gave us VIP treatment. We each got a little radio and a yellow headset so we could hear the crew chief and the spotter telling Joey what to do. Listening to the inside communication was a lot of fun.

Abbey was five years old at the time. She was obsessed with that yellow headset, but she was a little confused about how it worked. She thought Joey could hear her too. So she started talking to him. "Joey Wogano. Joey Wogano. Can you hear me, Joey Wogano?"

Joey was driving around the track at 185 miles per hour, and a five-year-old thought she was giving him instructions. We were all having so much fun watching her that none of us had the heart to tell her he couldn't hear her.

He has a crew chief and a spotter who talk to him while he's driving, and that's about it. Everyone else can yell and shout and cuss and cheer from a distance, but they don't get a direct line to his ear.

But what if they did? Imagine if Joey's team stood at the gate and told every fan, "Here's your radio and headset so you can say whatever you want to Joey. Any advice, any corrections, any trash talk. Have at it."

What if he could hear all those voices in his headset in real time? It would ruin Joey's focus. It would wreck his concentration. Nobody could race well with all those voices in their head.

And nobody can *live* well with all those voices in their head either. Nobody can face challenges with steadiness and courage if they let every critic and commentator be their copilot.

And yet, isn't that what a lot of us do? We give everybody a mic. "Here you go, CNN. Here you go, TikTok. Here you go, random internet troll with seventeen followers and a toxic attitude." Plus we're dealing with the loudest voice of all: the old self, the old you, who still tries to control everything.

I'm not saying it's wrong to listen to other voices if they're actually helpful, but they aren't your crew chief. They aren't your spotter. You can't afford to let every voice have the same access to your attention and your emotions.

Here's my point: To manage your *joy*, you have to manage your *focus*.

Earlier we talked about how Joshua had to lead Israel across the Jordan at flood stage. Before God did an upstream miracle for Israel, he had a heart-to-heart conversation with Joshua about focus.

> You can't afford to let every voice have the same access to your attention and your emotions.

Remember, Moses was gone now, and Joshua had recently been put in charge. That couldn't have been easy. Not only was he taking over from the only leader the nation had ever known, which meant everyone would be comparing him to Moses, but he also had to lead the people into situations that didn't make any sense and into battles that were bigger than anything they'd ever faced before.

I'm sure every general, commander, soldier, and citizen had an opinion about what they should do next. Joshua couldn't have all those voices in his head. So God gave him some advice about who he needed to listen to and what he needed to focus on.

> Be strong and very courageous. Be careful to obey all the law my servant Moses gave you; do not turn from it to the right or to the left, that you may be successful wherever you go. Keep this Book of the Law always on your lips; meditate on it day and night, so that you may be careful to do everything written in it. Then you will be prosperous and successful. Have I not commanded you? Be strong and courageous. Do not

be afraid; do not be discouraged, for the LORD your God will be with you wherever you go. (Joshua 1:7–9)

Notice two things here. First, God told Joshua to obey the law, keep it on his lips, and meditate on it. In other words, his actions, words, and thoughts needed to line up with faith, because for faith to be effective, it must be *focused*. Second, God told Joshua several times not to be afraid or discouraged but to be strong and *courageous*.

I think God was telling Joshua that his focus and his courage were connected. He knew Joshua was going to face a lot of risky, scary situations. He knew fear and discouragement were always going to be a temptation. He wanted Joshua to know that when negative emotions were trying to shut him down, when a thousand voices were telling him he was going to fail, he would need to focus his faith.

We need to do the same thing. We need to learn how to overcome fear and discouragement by focusing on what God says and doing what *he* tells us to do.

This doesn't come naturally for most of us. We don't focus our faith on God; we focus our fear on the problem in front of us. "I'm discouraged because I didn't make the team. I'm discouraged because my grades aren't getting any better. I'm discouraged because my parents keep fighting."

I'm not saying your problems are in your head. They are real, and they are challenging. It's normal to feel fear and frustration. But are you making them worse by listening

> It's normal to feel fear and frustration. But are you making them worse by listening to the wrong voices?

to the wrong voices? Are you letting fear be your crew chief? Have you made frustration your spotter? Maybe your discouragement is less about what you're facing and more about what you're telling yourself *about* what you're facing.

The Bible says that faith comes by hearing the word of God. The opposite is also true: Discouragement comes by hearing the words of the world, the whispers of worry, the arguments of anxiety. If you are dealing with fear and discouragement, pay attention to your dialogue. Not the dialogue you're having with others, although that can be part of it, but the dialogue you have on the inside. Notice if you're listening to the voice of fear, the voice of doubt, the voice of the old you.

God was saying, "Joshua, in order to be strong, in order to stay encouraged, you need to narrow your focus. Don't just go with whatever pops into your head or what people say you should do. Obey the Word, speak the Word, meditate on the Word. Focus your faith on the path I laid out for you, and you'll be successful."

Again, you're going to feel some anxious things, and that's okay. God wasn't trying to stop Joshua from *feeling* fear or discouragement. God wasn't saying, "Stop being so dramatic. Stop being so emotional. Stop crying or I'll give you something to cry about."

He didn't say, "Don't *feel* discouraged." He said, "Don't *be* discouraged."

There is a big difference to God between what you feel and who you are. Your condition is not your identity. Maybe you're feeling worried right now, but that's how you feel, not who you are. Maybe you're afraid right now, but that's your condition, not your identity.

GRAHAM

Labeling our identity with our emotions is something that I feel like I see my generation (myself included) struggle with daily. We tend to make excuses for our actions and blame them on who we are instead of how we might currently feel. I hear it all the time in the way we talk: "I'm an anxious person" or "I'm just depressed"—but these are feelings, not titles God has given us.

I tend to do this a lot with loneliness. As soon as I start to feel left out or not included, I call myself a lonely person. But the reality is, God has blessed me with amazing friends and family in my life. A lot of times our generation finds comfort in labels because then the problem doesn't require a solution. But as I grow into the true me, I have learned to control my feelings.

Before a wrestling match, it is very easy to let doubt creep in, but I have learned to speak things about myself that God says are true to combat that doubt instead of trying to find comfort in it.

It can be easy to let embarrassment creep in when I lead devotionals or Bible studies with my friends, but instead of labeling those things as embarrassing, I have learned to see them as opportunities to grow.

Flipping this switch in my brain from accepting labels to combatting lies has been one of the key factors in discovering who God says I am. He does not call me *anxious* or *lonely*, he calls me *free* and *chosen*.

God is not talking about a feeling here at all. He's talking about a focus.

He's saying, "It's okay that you feel it, but don't *be* it. Don't *behave* like it."

Self-talk can be brutal, so don't believe everything fear tells you. You don't have to accept the negative thoughts that pop into your head. They might not be true at all. They might not be the whole story. They might not be the right perspective. You need a security checkpoint in your brain, one of those TSA agents with no sense of humor at the entrance of your mind telling certain thoughts, "You're not coming past this point."

If you're not managing your mental focus, the enemy will try to sneak in and steal your hope. "Man, that situation is impossible. There's no way out of that." Or he's going to get you with worry. "I'll never get a job after I graduate. I'll never find someone who loves me. The world is terrible, and it's getting worse. We're all going to crash and burn."

I'm not trying to make you into some machine or say that you can always control what thoughts come in your mind, but you have more control than the enemy wants you to believe. You have to *choose* to focus, though, or you'll default to the old you.

If you're careful what you let in you, you'll be courageous when you face what's ahead. Be open to voices that help you, but don't elevate anyone to the level of God's Word. The Holy Spirit is your crew chief and your spotter. Listen to his voice. Meditate on it and obey it. Tell yourself what *he* says, not what fear, discouragement, or your Uncle Bubba says.

Where is God taking you? What has God told you? What is he speaking to you about the future? What is he asking you to do today? Make that your meditation, your declaration, and your occupation.

Don't give up what God gave you because of how you feel. Focus your faith, and be strong and courageous.

> ### ELIJAH
>
> I've never been the best about the way I talk to myself. Early on, I feel like I made a habit of roasting myself—jokingly at first—and it just got burned in as a pattern in my life. I rarely even realize I'm doing it.
>
> But recently, a friend told me they noticed I call myself an idiot a lot. He actually gave me like seventeen examples from times he's heard me say it.
>
> At first, my head went straight to, *Well, I get why that would sound weird, but I'm just joking when I say it.* And honestly, I think that's a dangerous place to be. Even if you're "just joking," don't you think your brain hears the way you talk to yourself? And let's not act like every human on the planet doesn't already struggle with having a positive self-image.
>
> So recently, I've been really working on not using negative words when I'm talking about myself. And when I do slip up, I try to cancel it out by saying, "No, I'm not an idiot," or whatever other negative thing I might have said. I feel like when we make a point to stop tearing ourselves down and start speaking life over ourselves, it actually helps us step into the person God made us to be.

TWENTY

A GR8FUL HEART IS A STABLE HEART

There's an old Chinese story I really love that is often called the "Parable of the Chinese Farmer." It goes something like this.

There was a farmer who lived in a small village in China. One day, his horse ran away. The villagers came by and said, "What bad luck!"

The farmer replied, "Maybe."

A few months later, the farmer's horse returned, and he brought a herd of wild horses with him. The villagers came to congratulate the farmer. "What good luck!"

The farmer answered, "Maybe."

Soon after, the farmer's son was trying to tame one of the wild horses, but he fell off and broke his leg. The villagers came to offer their sympathy. "What terrible luck!"

The farmer replied, "Maybe."

Then a war broke out in the region, and the emperor's soldiers came to the village to recruit young men for the army.

However, the farmer's son was exempt because of his broken leg. The villagers came by again. "What great luck!"

Again, the farmer responded, "Maybe."

That's how the story ends. It could go on forever—and that's the point. You can't really know if something is good or bad, at least not in the moment. All you can say is, "Maybe."

To me, this story teaches a powerful principle: You can't get your stability from your situation or let your environment control your emotions.

> You can't get your stability from your situation or let your environment control your emotions.

Why? Because you can't see past today. You don't know if the situation will change tomorrow. The thing you're griping and groaning about today may be the thing you're grateful for a month from now, a year from now, or ten years from now.

Now, the Chinese farmer could only trust in luck because bad things might turn out to be good things, and good things might turn out to be bad things.

Here's the thing, though: You don't trust in luck. Your faith is in a God who is present in your life and has good plans for your future.

I think that's what Paul had in mind when he wrote, "And we know that in all things God works for the good of those who love him, who have been called according to his purpose" (Romans 8:28). He wasn't saying your life will be free of pain, but rather that it's full of *purpose*, and even the difficult things will eventually work together for your good.

That means you don't have to worry and wonder if things are going to work out. You don't have to lose your mind when things go wrong. God's plans still stand, and sooner or later you're going to see his goodness.

The mindset that "My joy is my job" is based on that truth. It rests on the reality that even when my situation changes, my faith does not. It is focused on a God who knows the future and who will work all things together for good.

Of course, it's one thing to say, "God is working this together for good," but it's another to actually live that way in real time. Your mind can go from peace to panic in a moment. You can go from faith to frustration in two seconds flat. You might be happy and calm one moment, and the next you're saying, "I can't believe they did that again. This is horrible. This sucks. Why are people like this? Why is life like this?"

If your sense of well-being depends on the world around you, it's impossible to have a stable life because the world is not a stable place. You can watch twenty-seven videos in your feed and find twenty-seven reasons to believe everything is falling apart and the entire planet is headed to hell. You need a heavenly strategy to keep your emotions in check.

I didn't used to have a process to get my thoughts under control. For years, I saw myself as a victim of things that were happening on the outside rather than seeing myself as an architect of my surroundings. Instead of understanding what it means to have the mind of Christ, I was stuck in the mind of the flesh: the mental models and thinking patterns of the old me. If something bad happened, or if someone said something unfair or untrue about me, or if I made a mistake, it could mess me up for the rest of the day.

So here's the big question: How do you move from panic

back to peace? From frustration back to faith? From instability back to stability?

There are many tools and truths you can use, such as prayer, worship, reading the Bible, and talking with people who can help. But I want to focus on the strategy that, for me, seems to make the biggest and quickest difference.

Gratitude.

I know it's simple, but this is real-life stuff, not theory. It's something you can do when life hits you upside the head and you're saying, "I can't stop the bad thoughts from coming."

Don't try to stop them. Instead, stabilize.

And how do you stabilize? Gratitude.

It's the best intervention I've found when I need to bring spiraling thoughts and emotions back under my control. A thankful thought is one of the few things that can match the speed and power of negative thoughts. It does an end run around the negativity and gets you back to the goodness and grace of God.

> I can decide—at any point—to move away from anxiety or fear by practicing gratitude and faith.

This has been life-changing for me. It seems basic, maybe, but it has been so freeing to realize I can decide—at any point—to move away from anxiety or fear by practicing gratitude and faith.

I didn't come up with this strategy, of course. You can find gratitude journals on Amazon, gratitude affirmations on Spotify, and gratitude videos on TikTok. But it was in the Bible long before that.

For example, Paul wrote, "So then, just as you received Christ Jesus as Lord, continue to live your lives in him, rooted and built up in him, strengthened in the faith as you were taught, and overflowing with thankfulness" (Colossians 2:6–7).

Notice how he says "rooted," "built up," and "strengthened," which are stability terms, and then he adds, "overflowing with thankfulness." He's saying that stability and gratitude go together. Gratitude isn't the only way to be stable, but it's an important one, and often it's the easiest one to grab on to when you need a quick reset.

One exercise I often use is something my daughter, Abbey, and I came up with. It's one of the best things she's ever taught me, right alongside the hidden meanings in Taylor Swift's deep cuts. I'll quickly list—out loud if possible—eight things I'm grateful for right now.

Now here's the part Abbey showed me. She taught me to trace each of the fingers on my hand with a finger from my other hand as I list them. If you start on the outside of your pinky and go back down on the inside, by the time you get to your thumb, you'll be at eight. It's a physical act that reminds me that every good thing I have comes from God's hand.

Why eight? Because "eight" is right there in the middle of the word "grateful." See? GR8FUL.

I have other reasons too. In the Bible, the number *eight* is a symbol of new beginnings. If you turn 8 on its side, it looks like an infinity symbol. *Eight* is also the number of legs a spider has, and a spider can spin its own web from the inside. That's the secret of being content, of being strong, of not giving up: being able to find inside you what you need. You can spin something positive out of nothing. You can spin a better space to live in, regardless of your situation, because what you need is inside you, right where God put it.

Pick any eight things, as fast as they come to your mind. Don't analyze your entire past, present, and future and come up with the eight top things. Be more immediate and more specific than that. They can be the simplest things in the world.

The other day I said, "I'm grateful for my wife, who wants to go on a date with me tonight." I didn't stop for long, but I thought for a moment about where we might go. It shifted my energy.

"I'm grateful my shoulder didn't hurt this morning like it sometimes does." When you get to be my age, random body parts hurt for no reason. You find yourself thanking God not only for what feels good but also for what doesn't hurt as much as it did yesterday.

"I'm grateful Josh is coming over this afternoon to work on a project with me."

"I'm grateful the sun is out today."

"I'm grateful I get to drive my daughter to school in a few minutes and take her through Chick-fil-A."

"I'm grateful I get to share this message in a book that will help someone years from now."

"I'm grateful we have a family vacation coming up in a month and everyone seems excited to go."

"I'm grateful for..."

It's that easy. It takes three minutes at most.

The problem isn't finding eight—it's stopping at eight, because once you give your mind something to focus on, it keeps going in that direction all on its own. It might be a slow start, but notice Paul said, "*overflowing* with thankfulness." Once you turn on that faucet, faith keeps coming out. Favor keeps coming out. That's what you want. The goal is to get your mind out of a negative flow and into a positive one.

When you're in an overwhelmed state of mind, don't try to stop the avalanche of anxiety. Stabilize yourself with thankfulness. Give your mind something different to grab on to than the bad things that happened yesterday or might happen today.

> The goal is to get your mind out of a negative flow and into a positive one.

GRAHAM

As I said earlier, in wrestling, negative thoughts tend to fill my mind before I wrestle. The night before matches and tournaments, my mind begins to fill with negative thoughts about everything that could go wrong the next day. I will convince myself that my life is going to fall apart if I do not win this next match. This kind of thinking has caused me to not wrestle freely and to lose matches I shouldn't have.

One day, I asked one of my mentors, Jason Nolf, how he deals with nerves and anxiety before matches. He told me that at Penn State, where he wrestled, the number one thing they focus on is gratitude. He said before your matches, start to think about what you're grateful for and it will begin to destroy your anxiety and nerves.

I started doing this before every match. I would say things like: "I am grateful for the opportunity to wrestle. I am grateful for a family that loves me

> whether I win or lose. I am grateful for my teammates supporting me and pushing me to be better." Filling myself with positive thoughts of gratitude any time anxiety and fear creeped in has allowed me to wrestle much more freely.
>
> But this isn't just something I can use in wrestling. I can use this at school. I can use this when I feel left out or unappreciated. Combatting anxiety with gratefulness has definitely helped me in all areas of my life.

Now, keep in mind that gratitude is not the *only* way to deal with anxiety and other hard feelings, and there might be times you need to do more than a quick gratitude practice. I shared earlier that I see a therapist regularly, so I'm a big fan of using whatever strategies and resources work for you, including professional help.

Also, don't use gratitude to cover up real problems that need to be dealt with. If you need to deal with some stuff, deal with it. Don't use gratitude as an excuse to *hakuna matata* your way through life instead of putting in the work.

All I'm saying is that gratitude will help you stop a lot of dark thoughts and feelings before they can spiral into something deeper. This is street-fighting stuff. It's a strategy you can grab ahold of halfway through a class or while you're standing in line at the cafeteria, when your mind starts wandering down trails of negativity and you need to find a way back.

I picture my mind as being a little bit like our Boston

terrier, Bo. Bo is the dog Holly, Graham, and Abbey begged me to buy for them. It's also the dog that chewed through my favorite Ray-Ban sunglasses just the other day.

That brought up the question: How do you keep a dog from eating your sunglasses? You give him away to somebody else. Just kidding; my kids would kill me.

The real answer is to give him something else to chew on, something that was designed to be chewed on. You distract him by giving him something different to do.

I don't mean to compare your beautiful, capable brain to a Boston terrier, but I think the image paints a picture. If you don't manage your mind, it will start chewing on the wrong things. Negative things. Sad things. Fearful things. Hateful things.

Your mind doesn't need any help putting together a H8FUL list of all the things you don't like about your life. You have to give it a GR8FUL one instead.

Get your mind thinking about the goodness of God, the grace of God, the power of God who works all things together for your good. He is the source of what you have and what you need. You're not just grateful *for* things: You're grateful *to* the one who gave them to you. If he takes them away, he can give you more. There's stability in that kind of faith.

You might be used to a more pessimistic pattern of thinking, always finding what's wrong. Maybe you call that being realistic. But is that truly realistic? Or are you just letting the bad stuff control your focus? Even in hard times, there's always some good stuff happening too, but you have to look for it. If you don't overflow with thankfulness, you

> Even in hard times, there's always some good stuff happening too, but you have to look for it.

will probably have a mind that's overrun with anxiety and flooded with fear.

Let me share one more exercise with you. While it's great to thank God for the little things that come to your mind randomly, it's also good to focus on what you're *most* grateful for.

Recently, in one of my famous funks, when I couldn't seem to find a single thing that I was doing right in my life, I stumbled upon another gratitude strategy. It started with this question: *If I lost what I love the most, what would I give to have it back?*

The first thing I thought about, and the one I love the most, was God. But I can't lose my relationship with God. So I took it to the human level. If I lost Holly, my wife, who I love more than any other human being, what would I give to have her back?

The answer came instantly, automatically.

Everything.

I'd give everything to have her back.

Then what do I have right now? Everything. I already have everything. If I would give everything to have her back, and I have her, then I have everything.

Once I started thinking this way, the list kept growing. If I lost my kids, what would I give to have them back? Everything. I would spend every dollar, I would sacrifice every dream, I would go through any inconvenience. I'd give everything to have them back. I do have them, so I have everything.

It worked. Later that day, when the kids came home from school, I had a less annoyed perspective. Sure, they still fought and argued and made a mess at the table. But I realized that, even in that mess, there was a miracle that too many times I take for granted.

Now, maybe you *have* lost something you can't get back. I don't mean to bring you pain by including these comments. But even in the greatest loss, I'm sure there's someone or something that comes to your mind that you currently have. What does that relationship or blessing mean to you? And since you have it, how much do you have? How grateful can you be for it?

Beyond human relationships, you have forgiveness of your sin and peace with God. If you lost that, you would give everything to have it back. You have peace with God right now. You have forgiveness of your sin right now. So you have everything.

You have air in your lungs right now. If you lost your ability to breathe, what would you give to have it back? Everything. So with each breath, remind yourself, "I have everything I need in this moment. I have Jesus. I have life."

This doesn't mean that there aren't still unfulfilled desires. It doesn't mean that there aren't painful problems. It's just a perspective to stabilize you when the world seems to be crumbling around you. It's a strategy to give you back your joy.

You choose. Make the shift. The tools are yours to use.

A grateful heart is a stable heart, and a stable heart leads to a stable life. So do it right now. Think of your GR8FUL 8. Say them out loud if you can. Trace your fingers if it helps. Remember God's hand on your life.

> A grateful heart is a stable heart, and a stable heart leads to a stable life.

One…two…three…four…five…six…seven…eight. Go!

TWENTY-ONE

UGLY TRUST

A while back, Holly was out of town and I was bored, so I randomly Googled "concerts in Charlotte tonight." I thought I might catch one of my favorite nineties bands on a nostalgia tour, or maybe I'd find an indie rock show that would make me feel current.

Instead, I ended up at a Mendelssohn cantata, which is a performance of classical music with both voices and instruments. I was proud of how cultured I was. I even wore a suit.

When Holly called later that night, I told her, "You're not going to believe where I went all by myself."

She didn't believe it. Not only am I known for being an introvert when given the option, I'm way more comfortable at a rock concert than a symphony.

I was impressed by the musicians, and I had a good time. But there was one thing I couldn't get past: the entire cantata was in German. I didn't know that when I bought my ticket.

Now, I understand that classical music speaks to a lot of people on a subconscious and super-refined level that a punk rock guitarist like me could never understand. For me, though, half of my love of music is locked up in the lyrics. Sure, I could follow the emotional thread of the cantata through the music, but without a translation of the words, I missed a lot.

Why do I bring this up? Not to brag about how cultured I am—if anything, I think this story is proving the opposite. Rather, it's because I want to highlight a psalm that is very powerful and practical, but some of the beauty and message of the psalm is lost in translation.

The psalm is Psalm 34. From a lyrical standpoint, this psalm is a masterpiece. It's an acrostic poem. You can't see this in the English translation, but each verse starts with a different letter of the Hebrew alphabet. When you read it in English, you lose some of that grandeur. You're missing something, just like I did when I sat through Mendelssohn's cantata in German.

At its heart, this psalm is about trusting God *in real life*—not just when you're singing songs in church, not just when things are going well, not just when you feel spiritual and full of faith, but when the world seems to be falling apart around you.

Why does it matter that it's an acrostic? Two reasons. First, the message of this psalm must have been important to David because he put thought into it. He worked hard on it, and it shows. That means he wants us to take the message of this psalm seriously.

Second, it means this was not a spontaneous, real-time prayer because nobody prays through the alphabet when they're going through hell. You don't pray artistically organized prayers when you have four assignments due tomorrow and your computer keyboard just broke. You don't pray alphabetic prayers when your brother is screaming at your parents and they're screaming back. You don't craft prayers that are literary masterpieces when one of your friends is diagnosed with leukemia.

You cry out. You call out. You say exactly what's in your heart—and it's not pretty.

Now hang on to that thought for a minute, and let's look at what David wrote in Psalm 34 (KJV). These are just the first four verses.

> I will bless the LORD at all times; his praise shall continually be in my mouth.
> My soul shall make her boast in the LORD; the humble shall hear thereof, and be glad.
> O magnify the LORD with me, and let us exalt his name together.
> I sought the LORD, and he heard me, and delivered me from all my fears.

There are eighteen more verses that continue in the same tone. It's so majestic and elegant. So full of faith and joy. Even without being able to understand Hebrew, you can see the beauty here.

If you take this psalm at face value, you could almost get intimidated by how good David is at praise. But it's a little bit unrealistic, isn't it? Who talks like that when they're going through tough moments? Does anyone bless the Lord at *all* times? Or praise him *continually*?

That's a really high bar. I don't do that. I listened to my favorite rock band Metallica on the way to church the other day. It was early in the morning, I needed something to wake me up, and Mendelssohn just wouldn't cut it. I needed heavy metal to jump-start me. So I don't think praising God continually means playing only songs from Christian genres.

Not only does David say that he praises God continually, but he uses phrases like "I sought the Lord." I don't think I've ever used "sought" in a sentence. I don't ask Holly, "Hast thou seen my running shoes, my lady? I have sought them most diligently." When the dumb dog escapes from the house, I don't tell my kids, "Make haste to pursue the brute! Have you sought him at the neighbor's house?"

I don't talk in King James, and I definitely don't pray in King James when I'm going through painful moments. If I bump my toe on the coffee table, I don't say, "Oh, praise the Lord for a coffee table to bump my toe on. Some people in some parts of the world don't have coffee tables or the beans that make the coffee. I bless you for the beans and I bless you for the bumps." In moments like that, the word that comes to mind isn't "sought." It starts with "s" and ends with "t," but it isn't "sought."

Maybe you think trusting God should feel like poetry all the time, but you feel like cussing some of the time, and that doesn't seem spiritual at all. You know you're supposed to be joyful and content, but it's hard to praise God continually when you're just trying to survive.

That's okay. Don't let the devil tell you that your faith is fake just because your feelings are all over the place or you don't see a way forward.

You're putting the wrong kind of pressure on yourself. Because when I say, "My joy is my job," when I talk about how I should be full of God's peace and joy, that doesn't mean my process will always be pretty. Sometimes it's downright ugly.

You've heard of ugly crying? I call this ugly trust. And it's something David was really good at.

Sure, Psalm 34 is a literary masterpiece, but it didn't start that way—not even close. Here's the backstory.

David was not yet king. A few years earlier, he had killed Goliath, a giant from the Philistine city of Gath, and he had become a famous warrior and a hero of the people. That made Saul, the ego-driven, mostly insane current king, really upset, and he tried to kill David. So David fled for his life.

David went to Gath and met with their king, a man named Achish. At this point the Philistines got nervous because they didn't trust David. He had killed their hero, Goliath, after all, and he had been Saul's right-hand man. The people of Gath thought he was a threat, and rumors started flying.

I think that's interesting. David was running scared, but the enemy was scared of him. Do you know that your enemy recognizes you? Sometimes your enemy knows what you're capable of more than you do. That's not even my main point here, but it's worth remembering.

Anyway, David quickly realized his life was in danger. So he did the only thing he could think of to prove he wasn't a threat to anyone: He pretended to be insane. He scratched on the doorways and let spit dribble down his beard.

It worked. The king of Gath labeled him a lunatic and let him go.

Put yourself in David's place for a minute. Can you imagine how he felt? He was already under the greatest pressure of his life as he ran from Saul, and then it became even worse when he got to Gath. He was literally about to die. He could see people side-eyeing him and reaching for their swords. It probably wasn't hard to act crazy because he was at his emotional and mental breaking point already. Then, he had to add humiliation to the desperation. He sacrificed his dignity to escape with his life.

And that's the part of his life that David wrote this psalm about.

Not the part of his life where he was sitting under blue skies and an olive tree, strumming a harp. Not while gazing at sheep grazing by still waters.

He wrote it about the part of his life where had spit in his beard and splinters under his fingernails.

So that brings us back to the question: What does it really mean to say, "I sought the Lord"? Because David wasn't praying on his knees in the temple in this story. He wasn't reciting alphabetical poems or speaking with King James vocabulary.

He was hiding from Saul. He was humiliating himself before Achish. He was fleeing a madman and feigning madness, all while figuring out his next messy step.

Sometimes we talk so fancy about faith, but David was scratching gibberish on doorposts deep in enemy territory. That's what he was doing in the time he looks back on and writes, "I sought the Lord." We need to have a different definition for faith and trust in God. These things are messier and more practical than we think. And we might be better at them than we realize.

Seeking the Lord doesn't just mean going to church. It

doesn't just mean praying a prayer, singing a song, or reading a chapter in the Bible. It doesn't just mean you listen to worship music in your room or quote a verse a day to keep the devil away. I'm not saying you *don't* do those things, but you can't do those things all the time. Nobody can.

Some days, you're sitting alone at lunch, wondering if anyone notices you. You're staring at your phone, waiting for a message that never comes. You're watching your family fall apart and feeling helpless to stop it. When you pray in those moments, your prayers might not be pretty.

That's okay.

That's still faith. That's still trust. It's just ugly trust.

The devil might try to tell you that your faith isn't real because you're at your breaking point. I would argue that it's the most real it's ever been. You're in that space between calling out to God and seeing his answer.

That's a hard place to be. Remember, though, that one of the most beautiful psalms in the Bible came from one of the ugliest situations. Some of the most beautiful stories in your life will start with ugliness.

> Some of the most beautiful stories in your life will start with ugliness.

Ugly emotions. Ugly options. Ugly steps.

Ugly *trust*.

"Owning your emotions" doesn't mean thinking happy thoughts all the time. You're not Peter Pan trying to fly. It means you give yourself space to feel all the emotions, but you don't let them define you. You admit them but you don't submit to them. You feel *and* you trust. You fear *and* you believe.

And then you keep moving forward.

David sought the Lord *by* taking steps. In the middle of emotional chaos, his actions were the proof of his faith.

That's how you seek the Lord too. That's how you trust him. You do the next thing you can do, even when you wish you could do something different, trusting that God will guide you as you go.

Do you know what "ugly" stands for to me? *Until God Lifts You.* U.G.L.Y. I even have a verse for that. "Humble yourselves, therefore, under God's mighty hand, that he may lift you up in due time. Cast all your anxiety on him because he cares for you" (1 Peter 5:6–7).

Humility is trusting God to do what only he can do. He will lift you up in *due* time. So what will you *do* in the meantime?

You do the next thing. You don't have to figure out the next fifty things. That's God's job. Your job is to manage your emotions and take the next step.

Maybe you're stressed, but keep seeking. You're tired, but keep trusting. You're worried, but keep pushing forward, looking forward, taking steps of faith as best as you know how. It's road-weary, battle-scarred, tearstained, drool-down-your-chin trust, but it's still trust. It's still faith. It's still praise.

And soon, in due time, in God's time, you'll be able to sing with David, "I sought the Lord, and he heard me, and delivered me."

He will lift you up in due time.

What will you do in the meantime?

ELIJAH

Two things I've really tried to make a non-negotiable part of my day are praying and reading my Bible. My dad and I actually started a Bible club with our family to help keep each other accountable for reading the Word every day.

Just a few days ago, it was my turn to lead the Bible Club, but I had no energy to do it. I was ready to just skim, check it off the list, and move on. So that's what I did—I skimmed through it quickly to get it over with.

But as soon as I finished, I caught myself. I said, "No. Go back and read it right."

So, I went back. I slowed down. I actually took the time to read every verse carefully to see what God was really trying to speak to me that day. And it changed the whole trajectory of my day.

I've learned that it's not just about showing up when you want to—it's about showing up when you don't. Actually, it's *especially* about showing up when you don't want to. Because that's when you really get something from it.

Sometimes we overlook the fact that God didn't just create emotions—he *has* emotions. He is emotional, and we were made in his image. He is the perfect father who wants to help you get the most out of your emotions. That's the heart behind the mindset "My joy is my job." You can find stability and peace in God, and you don't need to deny your desires and feelings in the process. Your joy is your job, but your God is your source.

Your joy is your job, but your God is your source.

Knowing that, what's the next thing you can do *right now*? As we move into the sixth and final mindset, we're going to look at ways to "embrace your now." How do you take the next best step? How do you do the thing that you would do? This last mindset is one that will set you up for success in whatever season or situation you find yourself: *God has given me everything I need for the season I'm in.*

MINDSET (06)

GOD HAS GIVEN ME EVERYTHING I NEED FOR THE SEASON I'M IN.

ACTION STEP:
EMBRACE YOUR NOW.

TWENTY-TWO

LOOK TO THE LEFT

A while back I got a note from a man in my church named Trenton. Trenton is twenty-three years old, and he has cerebral palsy. He's a volunteer on the greeter team at our Lake Norman campus every other Sunday.

He wrote to tell me how much a recent sermon I preached and a song that we had written had encouraged him. The song was called "More Than Able," and in the sermon, I preached about God commanding Gideon to "go in the strength you have."

Trenton wrote, "I have a disability. That's how people define me. But when you preached about Gideon and you said, 'go in the strength you have,' I realized something. If you take the word *disable* and put *Go* in front of it, it spells 'God is able.' Even though I may be limited from a human perspective, God is able to do great things through my life."

That's a beautiful truth, and it meant so much to me. Trenton may have a physical limitation, but he has developed incredible spiritual strength. Where others see a disability, he sees God's ability—and that's what matters most. Trenton sees the fullest, truest perspective of himself.

Here's my question: Do *you* see the truest version of yourself? Do you see the ability of your God—or the disability of your doubt? Of your need? Your age? Your mistakes?

We all have limitations that we think could keep God from doing great things in our lives. Instead of letting them stop us, we need to let his "Go" turn whatever is disabled into "God is able."

Trusting God's grace in every moment is the heart of the mindset "God has given me everything I need for the season I'm in." Gideon experienced that grace, and many other heroes in the Bible did too. When God said "Go!" they stepped out in faith, and he provided what they needed at the right time.

I want to look at another hero in Judges who was perfectly prepared for his role: a man named Ehud. At the time Ehud showed up, Israel had been under Moab's control for eighteen years. They had to pay an annual tribute, and Ehud was in charge of carrying this tribute to the Moabite king, named Eglon.

The Bible says Ehud was a left-handed man. In that culture, left-handed people were often considered less-than-ideal soldiers. Ironically, Ehud was from the tribe of Benjamin, which literally means "son of my right hand." So in a sense, Ehud didn't fit into his own tribe, and he didn't meet other people's expectations of a warrior. He was a misfit.

Ehud was fed up with Moab's abuse of Israel, so he took matters into his own hands. Into his *left* hand, to be precise. When it came time to take the tribute to Eglon, he crafted a homemade dagger and hid it under his cloak, against his right thigh. Then he went to meet with King Eglon.

After Ehud handed over the payment, he told the king he had a secret message for him. So Eglon ordered everyone out of the room. Ehud came close to the king, reached across his body with his left hand, pulled out the dagger, and killed Eglon. The king didn't see it coming because it came from the left hand. Then Ehud locked the door, left the body where it fell, and sneaked out of an upper room.

How did he get out? Apparently by crawling down through the king's private toilet, which would have emptied into a chamber pot below. Then he escaped unseen. They might have smelled him, but they didn't see him. After his escape he got an army together, led a revolt, and freed Israel from Moab's power.

Now, I'm not saying that violence is the answer when you're dealing with mean people. Let me be clear about that. Remember, Israel was literally at war, and God had specifically called Ehud to fight for the freedom of his nation. (In other words, don't try this at home!)

Instead, I want to make a point: *God often does things in an unlikely way.*

In a secret way.

In a way nobody saw coming.

In a moment no one expected it to happen.

Using somebody no one thought could do it.

I want you to ask yourself: *What is the secret weapon God has put in my left hand? What is the secret weapon God is turning me into?*

In other words, what is the unexpected thing God wants

> What is the unexpected thing God wants to do through you?

to do through you? What is the unexpected way he wants to meet your needs? What is the unexpected skill he's given you? What is the unexpected situation you are going to be the solution for?

Maybe you're going through a tough time, and you think you know what needs to happen. Maybe you've even been praying very specifically, telling God how he could fix the issue. But what if you're looking at your situation the wrong way? What if you're expecting the wrong things? Maybe you're waiting for right-handed strategies (the way you think you're supposed to do it) but God made you left-handed (he created you to do it a different way). Maybe you already have what you need, but you have to think differently about yourself and what you can do.

I'm sure Israel thought they needed a leader with a foolproof battle strategy, a big army, and main-character energy. Instead, they got a left-handed loner with a DIY dagger and an escape plan borrowed from the Teenage Mutant Ninja Turtles.

Nobody saw that coming.

And that's why it worked.

Only Ehud could have pulled that off. And only you can pull off what God is calling you to do.

That's why you can't compare yourself to anyone else. You can't write yourself off by saying, "They're the right person, not me. Look how smart they are. Look how popular they are. Look who their parents are. Look at the car they got for their birthday. They're the obvious choice."

You don't know what God wants to do with you. Other people have all this stuff in their right hand that you don't have, but God has put something in your left hand, and nobody will see it coming. The enemy won't know what hit him.

Stop talking about what you don't have and start looking at what you do have. They might be "right" according to what is expected and normal and obvious, but if God is looking left, their right is wrong.

You have to believe that God is looking at *you*. He has prepared *you*. He is calling *you*. The misfit. The left-handed person from a right-handed tribe.

Don't diminish what makes you different. Destiny is often hidden in your difference. Maybe you have ADHD, or English is your second language, or you can't afford the right basketball shoes, or you're not the most outgoing person around, or you're dealing with some depression, or you grew up in a single-parent home. None of those things disqualify you. They might be exactly what God is going to use.

Stop trying to fit into expectations that God isn't putting on you. Stop trying to fit into molds that were never meant to fit you. And stop faking it for others instead of being who God called you.

The mindset "God has given me everything I need for the season I'm in" is about confidence in what God has given you and who God has made you *right now*. It's about stepping into what this season demands of you by being *who God made you to be*. That's what the true you would do.

Say it out loud, if you can: "God has given me everything I need for the season I'm in." Emphasize "everything" and "season" when you say it because those are the keys to this mindset. You have what you need for this season, so embrace your now. Get energized as you focus on what you *do* have and *can* do.

Ehud must have gotten energized at some point. He started looking around his house, trying to figure out what he could do with what he had, and suddenly he realized the left-handedness that people always laughed at was his secret strength. He drew up a plan worthy of a *Mission: Impossible* storyline, plotting his escape through a toilet because nobody would ever think to stand guard over a chamber pot.

It was genius. Gross, graphic, and gory, but still genius.

I wonder, what genius is hidden within you? What could you come up with if you looked around at what you have? If you redefined your quirks as qualities? If you took on a new energy and applied Holy Spirit creativity to whatever you're facing?

I'm not saying it's easy. I'm just saying you have specific skills and experience and knowledge, and God gave you those on purpose. He knew the seasons you'd go through, and he knew what you needed for each one—including the one you're in right now.

Now, when I talk about your left hand, I'm not just referring to using your unique strengths. That's part of it, but sometimes God uses your unique *weaknesses*. Or at least what you perceive to be weaknesses.

I'm not a boxer, but I took one lesson, one time, and one thing stuck with me. The instructor showed me that because I'm right-handed, I should lead with my left foot when I punch.

That seemed wrong at first. My left side is my weak side, so my left foot is weaker, right? It's less coordinated. It's less balanced.

But he explained that you pivot off your weak leg so you can punch with your strong hand. The power comes from the back. It comes from an unseen place, a place that doesn't seem strong on its own—but the power is in the pivot.

God will often lead with something that looks like weakness because our power is found in his pivot. He has us take steps forward, even in our weakness, then his strong hand does the work. I love what God told Paul when he was frustrated with his limitations: "My grace is sufficient for you, for my power is made perfect in weakness" (2 Corinthians 12:9).

Where are you stepping out and it feels like weakness? Where is God asking you to lead with the left? Maybe you're in a class that's way over your head. Or you're trying to be there for a friend but you don't know what to say. Or you're stepping up to lead a group project even though you're not the most confident speaker.

God's right arm will do the work. Just lead with the left. Lead with what you've got. "Whatever your hand finds to do," the Bible says, "do it with all your might" (Ecclesiastes 9:10). It might not feel like strength, but God's power is backing you up.

Your purpose will be clear when the time comes. God is sharpening and polishing you. He's getting you ready so that you'll have what you need when you need it.

Ehud had the weapon he needed for the battle God called him to fight. Ehud didn't just *have* a concealed weapon; he *was* the concealed weapon.

> The things God has put in you are not random, minor things. They are there for a purpose, and you are here for a purpose.

And so are you.

The things God has put in you are not random, minor things. They are there for a purpose, and you are here for a purpose. You are the weapon. You are the secret thing God is doing.

And you need to see yourself that way.

Timing matters, though. The prophet Isaiah compared himself to a secret weapon in Isaiah 49, but he also felt frustrated. Isaiah knew he was a weapon, but he also felt frustrated when he didn't see results. That's why he said, "I have labored in vain; I have spent my strength for nothing at all" (Isaiah 49:4).

Do you feel that way? Maybe it feels like you're putting in the work, but nothing is happening. You made yourself vulnerable trying to create relationships, but it backfired. You tried so hard to get over that health challenge, but nothing has improved. You struggled to break that addiction, but you keep going back to it.

Your effort feels like it was pointless because nothing changes, nobody sees you, nobody thanks you, nobody celebrates you.

But keep reading. Isaiah isn't done yet: "Yet what is due me is in the LORD's hand, and my reward is with my God."

Whose hand? *The Lord's hand.* The unexpected hand of God. The miracle you didn't see coming. The gift you didn't know he put in you. The door you almost didn't knock on, but you did, and it changed everything.

What is due you is in the Lord's hand because *you* are in the Lord's hand. Other people might have written you off. You might have written yourself off. But you're not forgotten. You're just hidden.

Don't let a lack of progress turn into self-pity. Self-pity feels good for a minute, but it discourages you. It steals your confidence and kills your creativity. It turns you into a victim when God is calling you into battle. It sabotages the strategic side of your mind, the problem-solving part that sees potential in hidden daggers and unguarded toilets.

You might be hidden, but things are still happening. God is doing something unexpected, something the enemy didn't see coming and won't be able to stop. You'll see it, and you'll be part of it, if you learn to look to the left.

TWENTY-THREE

HELP ME FAIL

One time a bodybuilder came over to my house, and he was working out with my boys and me in my home gym, the POUND. The guy was in his early twenties, and he was in the best shape of anyone I'd ever met. He brought his girlfriend along, who was also a bodybuilder. I figured I'd take the opportunity to ask him for some hacks so I could look like him—preferably ones that didn't involve human growth hormone.

He said something over and over that really got me thinking. When he was getting ready to do his last few reps on every set, he would say to his girlfriend, who was spotting him, "Help me fail."

It was so interesting to me that he said it that way. He didn't say, "Help me get one more rep" or "Help me set a new PR." He might have meant those things too, but what he said was, "Help me *fail*."

When you think of things you want people to help you do in life, that's not on the top of the list, is it? You don't text a friend and say, "Hey, I'm gonna ask so-and-so out, what should I say so that I get rejected?" You don't ask your basketball coach for pointers on how to miss more free throws. You don't get a math tutor and say, "Help me go from a C to an F."

That obviously wasn't the kind of failure this bodybuilder wanted. He wanted failure that would make him stronger on the other side.

I'm not a weight-lifting expert, but I've been lifting long enough to know that resistance training works by tearing down the muscle fibers and stimulating muscle growth and nerve connections. In this guy's weight routine, "Help me fail" meant "Help me get to the end of what I can do right now because that's where growth is going to happen."

Now here's my question: When you're facing pressures or problems that feel like a crushing, heavy weight, do you have faith that God could help you *fail*? Do you have faith that he is giving you what you need for this season, even when it feels like you're strained to the breaking point?

To be honest, I don't ever pray to fail. I say, "God, help me succeed. Help me win. Help me accomplish more."

It's okay to want to win. The Bible says that God leads us in triumph, that we are more than conquerors, and that we should run in such a way as to win the prize.

But winning doesn't always mean what we think it does. For God, character growth is a win. Perseverance is a win. Getting rid of old ways of thinking and acting is a win.

And sometimes to win, you have to fail.

Sometimes to win, you have to fail.

You have to go through things that break you down in order for God to build you up.

What does this have to do with the mindset "God has given me everything I need for the season I'm in"? Doesn't "everything I need" mean I'll never fail?

No—it means sometimes you need a *safe place to fail*, and God is that place for you. It means that in God, failure isn't fatal. It's not the end of the world, and it's not the end of what he'll do through you. Proverbs says, "For though the righteous fall seven times, they rise again, but the wicked stumble when calamity strikes" (24:16).

Often, we are too scared of failure. We think that getting to the end of ourselves is a terrible place to be because it's so uncomfortable. But for God, that's where growth begins.

You don't have to literally pray, "God, help me fail!" but you do need to know that you *will* fail—and even in failure, God is giving you all you need for the season you're in. He might be giving you what you need *through* your failure.

I hate that! I'm not going to lie and say I love to learn from my mistakes. As I said earlier, I'm a perfectionist at heart. I don't like failure. I wish I could get every decision exactly right on the first try. I wish I would never have to apologize for messing up again.

It's not going to happen, though.

So I'm learning to give myself space to grow in the safety of God's grace. I'm learning to recognize that even when I fail, God is enough and I am enough, because he's keeping me safe and helping me improve.

The Bible says, "We also glory in our sufferings, because we know that suffering produces perseverance; perseverance, character; and character, hope" (Romans 5:3–4). You don't feel strong when you fail—but when you fail, God makes you stronger. That's grace.

Now, I'm not talking about failing on purpose or making your suffering your identity. Don't do that. That's not helpful. There's enough failure built into the normal patterns of life. You don't have to go looking for it.

What I'm saying is that when problems and pain come your way, don't freak out too much. Don't overreact. Give yourself room to learn through trial and error, then come out stronger on the other side. Fail forward into your future.

When situations that feel like they're too much come your way, you can say, "God, help me fail, because I'm not getting it right in every area of my life. I'm not getting it right in the way I'm dating. I'm not getting it right in the way I'm relating to my parents. I made this decision, and it felt good at the time, but now it completely backfired. God, help me fail. Move me forward."

If you're heading into a situation this week where you feel like you're not enough, don't let fear of failure paralyze you. Maybe it's a person who you know is not going to accept you. Or a discipline you can't stick to yet like you want to. Or a project at school you've never done before. Or a schedule that is so full, you know you're going to let somebody down.

Whatever it is, *be more committed to progress than perfection*. Remember that you are being built up through the very things that feel like they're tearing you down.

Jesus called himself the Good Shepherd, but you could call him the

---
Be more committed to progress than perfection.

Good Spotter too, because he helps you fail. There is safety in his presence. He won't let you drop this weight. He's going to keep you safe and make you strong.

He's not going to carry it for you either, because you are enough for this. You have what you need for whatever you're facing. He's not only standing behind you, he's living inside you, and he's saying, "You've got this. I'm with you. This is making you stronger. It's building you back bigger. I'm giving you what you need for the season you're in, but you have to step into it. You have to accept the challenge. You have to push yourself to the limit, and if you fail, it's okay because I'm here to help you."

Remember Peter walking on water? Peter said, "Jesus, if you tell me to come, I'll come." Jesus told him to come, and Peter probably wished he'd kept his mouth shut. But to his credit, he gave it his best shot, and he did pretty well for his first attempt. He made it a few steps. And when his faith faltered, Jesus was right there.

People often criticize Peter for sinking, but he *walked on water* while the other guys stayed in the boat. He learned something firsthand that the other disciples only saw from a distance.

Notice something, though: Jesus didn't teach Peter a lesson about faith until *after* he tried to walk on water. He had to get wetter before he got wiser.

There are some lessons that can only be learned the hard way. Through mistakes. Through trial and error.

That's not a bad thing, though. Peter failed, but he learned—so he didn't actually fail. The sinking was temporary but the growth was permanent.

I think many of the greatest steps we take look a lot like Peter walking on water. We step out, we slip up, we call out, we learn something, and we try again. Meanwhile, other people sit in the boat and critique our technique. They are safe but stuck. They are dry but dormant. Wouldn't you rather sink a little today so you can grow a lot tomorrow?

Put yourself in a place where failure isn't just an option—it's a normal part of the process. Let God help you fail as you grow and grow as you fail.

> Let God help you fail as you grow and grow as you fail.

That means getting out of your comfort zone. It means doing things that feel difficult or unnatural. "I tried to make friends with that person, but it was so awkward. God, help me fail. I tried to apologize to my sister, but it didn't go very well. God, help me fail. I tried to stay calm in that situation, but I still got stressed out. Help me learn from my mistakes. Help me fail."

Don't fear your mistakes, your weaknesses, your limitations. If you let God be strong through them, you'll grow because of them. Failure done right is not failure at all. It's just another step forward as you do the true you.

TWENTY-FOUR

FOUND FISHING

I listen to a lot of motivational speakers and fitness gurus while I'm driving or working out, and they always talk about how the right morning routine can set you up for success. One morning, not too long ago, I was feeling a little anxious. So I started going through a list of all the morning routines and rituals I had heard about that are supposed to get you on track for the day. I wrote them down, and by the time I finished the list, I had to laugh at myself. I thought, *I need to stop watching YouTube videos and listening to audiobooks about morning routines. This is out of control.*

If I did all those things—breathing exercises, biblical meditation, exercise, silence, cold and hot showers, prayer lists, acts of generosity, a balanced breakfast, vitamin supplements, to-do lists, gratitude journals—I wouldn't finish my morning routine until three in the afternoon.

I felt God speak to me, though. "Steven, you have a lot of things that could get your mind to a better place. Pick one. Do one."

Pick one. Do one.

It's a simple thought. But it's a powerful one. If you're feeling stuck, moody, worried, confused, or ashamed—what is one thing you could do to get yourself back on track?

It comes back to the idea of "do the thing that you would do." You can't do everything, but you can pick one thing and do it.

That's how you embrace your now: by accepting where you are and doing what you can with what you have. Maybe it's just a quick tweak to your attitude before you head off to school. Maybe it's reaching out to someone you know will give you good advice.

Pick one. Do one.

Choices like these *are* faith. Faith doesn't mean you know everything that's going to happen or that you're sure about what to do next. It means you're faithful with what you have right now by putting yourself in a place where God can find you, encourage you, use you. I wouldn't call it meeting him halfway—it's more like meeting him about 5 percent of the way in. But that 5 percent matters. It's your faith in action. It's proof you believe that God is with you and that he has given you what you need in this season.

When I don't know what to do in a confusing situation, I remind myself that when I make a move, God makes it clear. I'd prefer it the other way around—I want God to make it clear, then I'll make a move. But it often doesn't work that way.

> **When I make a move, God makes it clear.**

Are you in that place right now? Maybe you're saying, "What can I do? What should I do? I just don't know."

I've been there. We all have, many times. Sometimes all it takes is a bad mood, a bad decision, or some bad news, and suddenly you're feeling overwhelmed and hopeless. You didn't get into the degree program you were planning on. Your mom lost her job at the worst time. Your best friend just told you they're moving away.

How do you respond when you don't see a path forward? How does the *true you* respond? Because that's the version of you that you want to listen to.

The old you might have frozen up. It might have fallen into self-doubt or self-pity. But the true you asks, "What can I do right now? What has God shown me? I'm going to pick one thing and do it."

Maybe you've read the story in John 21 about how Peter went fishing after Jesus' death and resurrection. He invited some of the other disciples along, and they fished all night.

Early the next morning, Jesus appeared to them. He even cooked them breakfast. Then he started talking to Peter.

Remember, after Jesus was arrested, Peter had denied three times that he even knew him. Now, as they stood next to the fire, Jesus asked Peter three times if he truly loved him. He also told him three times to feed his sheep, which meant to take care of the people God would put under his leadership. It was a dramatic, emotional scene.

I've heard people criticize Peter for going fishing, because that was his job before Jesus called him. I've heard preachers say that he gave up and went back to his old way of life and he dragged other people with him.

I don't think that's true, though. I don't think he went fishing out of fear. I think he was fishing in faith.

He wasn't giving up. He was reaching out.

Think about it. I'm sure he was emotionally raw. After all, he had denied Jesus in front of everyone, then he ran away and hid when Jesus and the disciples needed him most. He completely failed at his leadership role. But he wasn't the kind of guy to sit around doing nothing, so when he didn't know what else to do, he did what he was doing when Jesus first called him to be his disciple—he went fishing.

Remember, Peter had seen a lot of miracles around this lake. It's where he cast his net on the other side of the boat and caught so many fish that his nets began to break. It's where Jesus came to his disciples walking on the water, and Peter even took a couple of steps on the water himself. It's where Jesus told Peter, when he was worried about paying taxes, to go catch a fish, and that fish came out of the water with money in its mouth.

So when Peter went back to his boat after Jesus' death and resurrection, I think he was fishing in faith. When he was caught in a place between failure and calling, between fear and his future, between who he used to be and who he knew he was meant to be—he went fishing.

And Jesus found him fishing.

Can you relate to Peter? Maybe you're saying, "I've made mistakes. I made wrong choices. I don't know if God can still use me. I don't know if God really forgives me. I'm not as strong as I thought I was. What do I do?"

What if you said, "I want to be found fishing"? What if you said, "I don't know what to do, but I'm going to do the thing that puts me closest to where I've met God before"?

When Peter did what he knew, Jesus did something

new. Not only did he restore Peter, gently and firmly, but he expanded his calling. "Feed my sheep," he said. The encounter with Jesus happened *because* he went fishing. Jesus showed him the next steps after Peter took the first step.

Here's the point. When you feel confused or overwhelmed by something you're facing, don't freeze up. Don't get analysis paralysis. You don't have to understand every detail or see every step ahead.

Instead, go fishing.

What does that mean? It means doing what you know you should do, even when—*especially* when—you don't have control over everything else in your life. What things do you already know how to do? What things do you have at hand? What do you know God wants you to do now?

Pick one. Do one.

Sometimes this means taking a big step forward, but often it's just an attitude change. That's why I mentioned morning routines that get your mind and emotions in the right place. I'm not saying you need a specific routine—I'm just saying that even when you're overwhelmed, you have options. You don't always get to choose how your day flows, but there are ways to start off on the right foot. And if things go sideways, there are ways to stop and reset.

> Even when you're overwhelmed, you have options.

For Peter, that was fishing. For me, it's often practicing gratitude, such as the Gr8ful 8 exercise I mentioned earlier. "I'm grateful for the time I had with Elijah lifting weights today. I'm grateful Graham and I got to watch wrestling this weekend. I'm grateful Abbey gave me a hug and told me she loved me last night. I'm grateful Holly and I are going on a walk today, and for once it's not twenty-two degrees out."

When I do that, suddenly the day has a different feeling. All because I went fishing for gratitude. I went fishing for faith. I went fishing for a change in perspective. I found *them* fishing, and Jesus found *me* fishing.

How about you? How do you get unblocked? How do you move from pessimism to possibility? From resenting your now to embracing it? Where do you hear God best? What's one thing you could do *right now* to get closer to him and closer to the true you that he's guiding you into?

In other words, how could you go fishing?

If you don't go fishing for the right things on purpose, you'll likely end up fishing for the wrong ones by default. If you fish for reasons to give up, you'll catch them. If you fish for discouragement, you'll find it. If you fish for excuses, they'll bite quickly.

But on the other hand, if you fish for kindness, you'll find that too. If you fish for reasons to believe, or if you fish for the best in people, or if you fish for the next thing that God is giving you to do, you'll get it.

You get what you fish for, not what you wish for.

So go fishing and see what you catch. See what God does. See what he shows you.

That means taking time to find out what God wants you to do next, no matter how small it might seem. Some of us spend more time looking for something to watch on Netflix than we do figuring out God's will for us today. When was the last time you got alone with God and asked him for a strategy to get you moving again? When was the last time you opened your Bible for wisdom instead of TikTok? When was the last time you asked somebody in your life for help? Are you spending all your time telling God how hard this is going to be and how big the situation you're facing is, or are you telling your situation how big your God is?

Instead of sitting around feeling bad about your failures or worrying about what's coming next, get up and go fishing.

Jesus will find you there. He is reminding you, "I'm glad you're going to be out on that boat because that's where I'm going to be this morning. I'm going to be on the lake looking for somebody who's doing what they know to do so I can show them who they really are."

God has given you everything you need for the season you're in. Don't stress or obsess over every possible thing that could happen tomorrow. Work on today. Get in your boat today. Look for Jesus on the waters of faith today. Embrace your now and be found fishing.

> **God has given you everything you need for the season you're in.**

TWENTY-FIVE

GOD CHOSE YOU ... WILL YOU?

Side by side in my refrigerator, I have bottles of water and Diet Coke. Every day, I get to choose which one to put into my body. Usually I go for Diet Coke, if I'm being honest. Don't judge me.

Side by side on my phone, I have my Bible app and my YouTube app. I get to decide where to put my focus and time. It's my choice.

Side by side in my mind, I have thoughts that encourage me and thoughts that paralyze me. There's a voice that says, "You have something to say. You can help people. You can encourage people." And there's another voice right next to it that says, "You don't have everything all figured out. Who are you to tell people how to live?" I choose which voice to listen to. It's up to me.

And side by side, there is my old self and my new self. The fake me and the true me. The me I've always known, and the me God knew since he created the world.

Which me will I choose today? Which you will *you* choose today?

I don't think we have a clue how much choosing we actually do in a given day. Our lives are built around the little decisions we make along the way. Earlier I quoted Psalm 118:24. "This is the day the LORD has made. We will rejoice and be glad in it" (NKJV). God made the day I'm living—but I choose what to make of it.

> God made the day I'm living—but I choose what to make of it.

The power of choice is the heart behind all six of the mindsets we've been exploring together, and it's the heart behind the action step "Embrace your now." You can't control most things, but you can control the most important things: your mind, your emotions, your words, your reactions, your decisions, your internal dialogue.

Most of the choices we make are small and almost instantaneous. When I see my kids in the morning, *I choose* whether to greet them enthusiastically or whether to be distracted or grumpy. (To be honest, I'm not always great at this.) When I talk to someone I work with, *I choose* whether to begin with, "Hey, I'm excited about…" or whether I skip right to something I'm frustrated about. When I think about everything I have to do today, *I choose* if I'm going to look at those things through negativity or possibility.

When I first wake up, my breath isn't the only thing that's bad. My attitude is bad. So are some of my emotions and thoughts. I have to get my head in the right place or I'll have a meltdown by ten o'clock. If I don't adjust my mindset in the morning and believe that "God has given me everything I need for the season I'm in," I'll run around feeling like I don't have enough strength, I don't have enough energy, I don't have enough time.

Which version of you are you sending into the world every day? Is it the one that will get you where you want to go in your friendships? In your mental health? In your education or career? In your walk with God? Are you choosing to be who God says you are and do what God says you can do, or do you sometimes settle for immaturity in the name of authenticity? Are you stuck in the old self when God is calling you to step into your true self?

Now, I'm not telling you to obsess over every choice you make. You make thousands of decisions a day, and you're not going to get them all right. I'm just saying that the launchpad for *doing* the true you is *choosing* the true you. It's accepting who God made you and then making the daily—sometimes hourly—decision to walk in the best version of that.

We've spent this entire book exploring how to do this. Each mindset is a tool, a strategy, so you can choose the next best step even when life is confusing or overwhelming.

Choosing yourself must start and end with the fact that *you are chosen by God in Christ*. Ephesians 1:4 says, "For he chose us in him [Christ] before the creation of the world to be holy and blameless in his sight."

> Choosing yourself must start and end with the fact that *you are chosen by God in Christ.*

God didn't just know you before he created you. He *chose* you before he created you. And remember, God has options. God can use anybody he wants—and he picked you.

The Bible calls us "chosen vessels." That means you are a hand-picked vessel of God, even if you feel kind of cracked. Even if you feel a little stubby or if you think your shape is not right, or you're too tall or short or awkward or funny-looking. You're a chosen vessel, even if you have a broken handle.

The poet and singer Leonard Cohen said there's a crack in everything, and "that's how the light gets in."* Our weaknesses and our cracks are where God's grace and glory shine through. That's where God does his best work.

Sometimes we get obsessed with the container—with our bodies, our skills, our accomplishments, our grades, our influence—but God sees right through those things. They aren't deal-breakers at all. They are part of our beauty.

Now, those things have value, and you need to take care of yourself. But if you're going to work on those things in a healthy, balanced way, you have to know deep down that God chose you.

"Yeah, but I'm not…"

You're *chosen*.

"But I did that…"

You're *chosen*.

"It's just that they…"

You're *chosen*.

You've been selected and accepted by a God whose sovereignty surpasses every situation and every human limitation. You are the handiwork of the architect of time and space and

---

* Leonard Cohen, "Anthem," *The Future* (music album). Songwriters: Leonard Cohen; Anthem lyrics © Stranger Music Inc. (1992).

galaxies. The God who designed the caterpillar to become a butterfly created you for good works. He called you for a special purpose. He adopted you as a son or a daughter. He brought you into his family.

That's good news, isn't it? It means 5'6" was supposed to be 5'6". It means your brain is wired the way it is because he's going to use that for his purposes. It means that beneath whatever you don't like about yourself radiates a spirit that isn't messed up by comparison to others.

God called you to this time, to your family, in the place you live, with the personality he gave you. That's all part of his purpose. Remember, he chose you before the creation of the world, and that means he chose you before life got messed up or you got messed up.

He chose you before that breakup. He chose you before you had those wrong relationships. He chose you before you got trapped by that addiction. He chose you before you made that mistake. He chose you before you were abused by that person. He chose you before you blew that opportunity.

God chose you—*but you have to choose yourself.*

> God chose you—*but you have to choose yourself.*

Stop rejecting who you are or who you are not. Stop comparing yourself to people you don't even know. Believe what God says about you. Decide to act like the person he says you were created to be and step into the calling he created for you.

We already saw that you were "created to be like God in true righteousness and holiness," as Ephesians says, but you have to reach for it, moment by moment, in every situation. I don't mean that you have to earn it; I mean you reach for it like you're receiving a gift from God, or like you're getting a Diet Coke out of the fridge. Or a bottle of water, if you're in a healthy mood.

What do you need to reach for and receive? And to do that, what do you need to release and leave behind?

God chose you, so you have to let go of the reasons why he shouldn't have. You have to stop listing all your excuses for why he can't use you.

Remember how God told Moses to deliver his people from Egypt, but Moses said he couldn't speak well enough? Or how God told Gideon he would save his people, but Gideon said he was the weakest warrior in all of Israel? Or when God said Sarah would have a child, but she laughed out loud in unbelief? They were holding so tightly to their excuses that they struggled to receive God's power.

You and I do that sometimes. "I don't have the time. I don't have the money. I don't have the skills. I don't have the intelligence. I don't have the background."

Release that and reach for what God has given you. Choose to believe who God says you are. "I choose to believe that Jesus made me righteous. I choose to believe that the Holy Spirit lives within me. I choose to walk in it. I choose to flow in it. I choose to turn the other cheek in this situation. I choose to walk past that insult. I choose to forgive. I choose to speak life. I choose to go forward."

This isn't always easy. It's definitely not instantaneous. I struggle with this, and I'm sure you do too. I choose the horrible attitude sometimes. I choose the gossip, which feels good in the moment but then leaves me feeling gross because I can't look people in the eye if I've been talking badly about them behind their backs. But I recognize that's not the me I want to be at all. I don't want to be the bad-attitude me, the gossiping me, the mean me.

I want to be a bigger me. I want to be big enough to look at somebody and see that they have pain, they have feelings, they have reasons, they have dreams, they have goals. I want to see people as people, not as problems to solve or tools to use. I want to see the gifts in my friends rather than getting sidetracked by the little things that trip me up in their everyday behavior.

That's who I want to be, but I have to choose to be it. I have to choose me.

And you have to choose you. You have to settle deep in your soul that God saved you, God loves you, God is for you, God is with you, God has called you, God is guiding you, God is changing you.

Will you choose yourself?

Will you choose not to abandon yourself to the addiction? Will you choose to reach out to somebody you love today rather than isolating yourself? Will you choose to move forward on that big dream you have, even if it's just a tiny step in the right direction? Will you choose the future instead of the past? Will you choose to be present instead of being distracted? Will you choose growth even when it's hard work?

Maybe you're in a place where you want to quit on yourself right now. But if God won't give up on you, you don't get to either.

If Jesus went all the way to the

> If God won't give up on you, you don't get to either.

cross for you, if he pushed past the pain and ridicule and then sat down at the right hand of God, you can endure as well.

It may take a little longer than you hoped. It may hurt a little more than you expected. But the God who chooses you is asking *you* to choose you today.

He knows what you're going through, but he also knows what you're capable of. He knows what you're missing, but he also knows he has given you what you need for the season you're in.

Maybe you can't see everything he has planned for you, but you step into it, one decision at a time.

God chose you. Will you?

When we say, "God has given me everything I need for the season I'm in," it doesn't just point to today—it points toward the future. You have enough for today *and* you'll have enough for tomorrow. Regardless of what's around the next bend in the road, you'll have enough and be enough.

God already knows the season you'll step into tomorrow. He knows the challenges you'll face a year from now. He knows the doors he's going to open in ten years. You might not, but he does, and his provision will be there when you get there.

CONCLUSION

STEP BY STEP, DAY BY DAY

I was talking with a friend of mine recently, and he said, "Man, isn't it supposed to get easier at this point in our life? Is it still going to be this much of a battle every day?"

I knew what he meant. When I was a teenager, I assumed that by my thirties or forties, I'd have things figured out. My biggest battles would be behind me, and the future would be clearer. Having the right attitude would come naturally. Doing the right thing would be easy.

Turns out I was wrong.

Turns out there are always some unexpected challenges around the next bend. Turns out there are still things about myself that can and should change. There are mistakes I need to make, skills I need to learn, "demons" I need to deal with, and doors I need to walk through with courage and tenacity.

Turns out God isn't done with me yet.

And he's not done with you either. He's just getting started.

That's an awesome thought. It means you aren't locked

into your present. There are mountains to climb and battles to win and dreams to fulfill.

Psalms says that God's thoughts toward you outnumber the grains of sand and that your future is written in his book. That means he has a bigger vision for you than you do. He trusts you more than you do. He believes in you more than you do. And he won't give up on you like you sometimes do.

Remember, though, as you grow into the true you, there is a lot riding on the voices you let into your head. Your stability and your inner peace depend on whether you tune in to God's voice above all the noise, or whether every rumor, threat, and random negative thought has access to your ear.

The wrong voices are the ones that don't know the true you but still think they can tell you who you are and how much you're worth. They are the voices that point out your problems and magnify your mistakes, not to help you grow, but to hold you back. To lock you into the version of you they have always known, instead of encouraging you to grow into who God made you.

Sometimes those voices are real people. Other times, they are internal voices. They are memories. They are imaginations. They are insecurities. They are mindsets you've learned over time. They are tricks for kids, lying lizards, dead weasels.

The six mindsets that we've explored in this book are meant to replace those voices. Instead of listening to the things that hold you back, you have the power to change your inner dialogue and to adopt a God-focused mindset. No matter what challenge or battle or opportunity you face, you can do the thing that the true you would do, because that is the real you.

The old you might have been swayed by wrong voices, but the true you is learning to focus on the voice of God. You are learning to listen to the one who knows you best and sees you as you were created to be.

Let's look at the six mindsets one more time. If you can, say these six mindsets out loud to yourself, one at a time, with all the confidence and faith you have. This is the voice of the true you. This is the way the true you thinks, speaks, and acts.

1. *I'm not stuck unless I stop.*
   Action Step: Commit to progress.
2. *Christ is in me. I am enough.*
   Action Step: Accept your Self.
3. *With God there's always a way, and by faith I will find it.*
   Action Step: Focus on possibility.
4. *God is not against me, but he's in it with me, working through me, fighting for me.*
   Action Step: Walk in confidence.
5. *My joy is my job.*
   Action Step: Own your emotions.
6. *God has given me everything I need for the season I'm in.*
   Action Step: Embrace your now.

I hope you'll put these six mindsets in your phone or write them on sticky notes and post them in your room. I hope you'll read them when you need them most.

Sometimes they won't feel true. Sometimes they'll seem

like wishful thinking. But these are the words God has spoken over your life. They are as true in the valley as they are on the mountaintop. They are as true when you're doubting as they are when you feel certain. Hear the Holy Spirit whispering them into your heart right now.

God is with you and for you.

He sees you and he chose you.

He knows you, loves you, believes in you, provides for you.

And with his help, you can do the true you.

ACKNOWLEDGMENTS

Justin Jaquith, you were the ideal creative collaborator to bring this book to life with me. You possess a rare combination of big-picture consciousness and relentless meticulousness. You dove to the bottom of the Basin. And you did it the right way, which wasn't the easy way, until we discovered and captured the energy and essence of this message. Thank you for being tenacious and patient, flowing with a preacher, and staying all in, to the end.

Shannon Marven, you expanded my concept of what an agent can be. You brought a level of support and nurture that comes only from someone who cares deeply. Thank you for really believing in me and helping me get through precious and break through to personal. Jan Miller, thank you for your vision and commitment to my next step.

Daisy Hutton, Beth Adams, Patsy Jones, and the team at FaithWords, I am excited to be publishing with you. You are excellent partners.

Lindsey Newton, you are an anointed archivist. Thank

you for stewarding the recording and distribution of my sermons faithfully for so many years.

Lindsey Pruitt, Chad Zollo, Cherish Rush, and Christy Collins, I wish every pastor could have a team like you. Thank you.

Chunks Corbett, I know you probably won't read this whole book, but hopefully you get this far, because if not for you, it wouldn't exist. Thank you for never letting me forget this is part of my calling too. Thank you for every time you've blocked for me so that something creative could be born.

Danielle Axelrod, I knew you were the key to getting this completed at the highest level. No one else could have wrangled all the participants and woven all the elements so skillfully. Thank you.

Holly Anna, you insisted there were more books in me, and you did more than say that. You made sure I found my next one and made sure it didn't stay inside. That's what you always do. Thank you. You are the greatest gift God ever gave me.

Elijah, Graham, and Abbey, not only did the best illustrations in this book come from your lives, but you contributed some of the best insights. Thank you for helping me break it down and flesh it out. Thank you even more for being the reason I wanted to write this. I'm proud of you. "Why you scrolling through the old pictures?"

ABOUT THE AUTHOR

STEVEN FURTICK is a pastor, *New York Times* best-selling author, and Grammy-Award-winning songwriter and producer. As founder and senior pastor, he has helped grow the multi-site Elevation Church into a global ministry through online streaming, television, and the music of Elevation Worship. He holds a master of divinity degree from Southern Theological Seminary and is the author of six previous books. His three children, Elijah, Graham, and Abbey, collaborated with him on this project, offering personal experiences and applications along the way. The Furtick family lives in Charlotte, NC.